DATE DUE			
May 13 '71			
Mar 3 '72			
May 25 72			
Mar 20 80			
GAYLORD M-2			PRINTED IN U.S.A.

BAIT CASTING

The Barnes Sports Library

ARCHERY
ARCHERY by Reichart and Keasey

BADMINTON
BETTER BADMINTON by Jackson and Swan

BASEBALL
HOW TO PITCH by Feller
BASEBALL by Jessee
THE DICTIONARY OF BASEBALL WITH OFFICIAL RULES by Cummings
BASEBALL TECHNIQUES illus. by Allen and Micoleau

BASKETBALL
DRILLS AND FUNDAMENTALS by Bee
MAN-TO-MAN DEFENSE AND ATTACK by Bee
THE SCIENCE OF COACHING by Bee
ZONE DEFENSE AND ATTACK by Bee
BASKETBALL ILLUSTRATED by Hobson
BASKETBALL by Murphy
BASKETBALL FOR GIRLS by Meissner and Meyers
BASKETBALL OFFICIATING by Tobey

BOWLING
BOWLING FOR ALL by Falcaro and Goodman

BOXING
BOXING by Haislet

CHEERLEADING
CHEERLEADING AND MARCHING BANDS by Loken and Dypwick

FENCING
FENCING by Vince

FIREARMS
RIFLE MARKSMANSHIP by Stephens

FISHING
HOW TO TIE FLIES by Gregg
BAIT CASTING by Robinson
BASS BUG FISHING by Brooks
FLY CASTING by Robinson
STRIPED BASS by Rodman
SURF FISHING by Evanoff

FOOTBALL
FOOTBALL by Killinger
TOUCH FOOTBALL by Grombach
SIX-MAN FOOTBALL by Duncan
FOOTBALL TECHNIQUES illus. by Moore and Micoleau

GAMES
LAWN GAMES by Tunis

GOLF
GOLF ILLUSTRATED by Berg and Cox

HANDBALL
FUNDAMENTAL HANDBALL by Phillips

HOCKEY
FIELD HOCKEY FOR GIRLS by Lees
ICE HOCKEY by Jeremiah

JIU-JITSU
JIU-JITSU by Lowell

PHYSICAL CONDITIONING
PHYSICAL CONDITIONING by Stafford and Duncan

RIDING
RIDING by Boniface
RIDING SIMPLIFIED by Self

ROPING
ROPING by Mason

SELF DEFENSE
SELF DEFENSE by Brown

SKATING
ROLLER SKATING by Martin

SKIING
SKIING by Prager

SOCCER
SOCCER by Fralick
SOCCER AND SPEEDBALL FOR GIRLS by Hupprich

SOFTBALL
SOFTBALL by Noren
SOFTBALL FOR GIRLS by Mitchell

SQUASH RACQUETS
SQUASH RACQUETS by Debany

SWIMMING
SWIMMING by Kiphuth

TENNIS
TENNIS by Jacobs
TENNIS MADE EASY by Budge
PADDLE TENNIS by Blanchard

TRACK AND FIELD
TRACK AND FIELD by Conger

VOLLEY BALL
VOLLEY BALL by Laveaga

This library of sports books covers fundamentals, techniques, coaching and playing hints and equipment, uniformly priced at $1.50. Leading coaches and players have written these volumes. Photographs and drawings illustrate techniques, equipment and play.

BAIT CASTING

GILMER ROBINSON, M.S.

DEAN OF MEN AND ASSISTANT PROFESSOR OF PHYSICAL
EDUCATION, KALAMAZOO COLLEGE, KALAMAZOO, MICHIGAN

A. S. BARNES & COMPANY

NEW YORK

PRINTED IN
THE UNITED STATES OF AMERICA

DEDICATED

TO THE BOYS OF

CAMP NEBAGAMON

ACKNOWLEDGMENTS

Acknowledgment is hereby gratefully made to the many fishing tackle people who have contributed materials for this publication. Much credit is due Mr. Davis and Mr. Tony Accetta for reading and giving helpful criticism of the manuscript. The author wishes to express his appreciation to Robert Maunder for the drawings and diagrams that are used, to Mr. S. R. Townsend for reading and correcting the manuscript and to the many fishermen whose experiences helped make this publication possible.

FOREWORD

THE NOVICE FISHERMAN and the experienced fisherman who would like to have additional information on the art of bait fishing will find this book very interesting and instructive in explaining different methods which I have used and taught in my thirty-five years of fishing and tournament work.

TONY ACCETTA.

U. S. Professional Bait and Fly Casting Champion.

CONTENTS

Foreword   ix

I.   Fundamentals of Casting   1

II. The Beginner's Equipment   13

III. Tips on Fishing   24

IV. Bait   30

V.   Fresh Water Game Fish   39

VI. The Sport of Bait Casting and Fishing   58

     Index   65

~~~~~~

CHAPTER I

FUNDAMENTALS OF CASTING

PATIENCE AND PRACTICE inevitably form the background of any fine
exhibition of skill in sport, and this is also true in bait casting. But
the sometimes long hours of practice are more than made up for by
the ability to put your bait in the exact spot where you want to,
adding the joy of skillful marksmanship to the fun of fishing. Aside
from the pleasure of handling one's tackle proficiently, there is also
the satisfaction of being able to try all the most likely spots, for the
best fishing places are sometimes hard to reach—underneath overhanging branches, close in to shore, or close by weeds and lily
patches.

One of the reasons fishing enthusiasts have not been more successful is that they have not bothered with the fundamentals of good
casting. Unless a person takes the time to learn them, he can never
hope to become very proficient in the art of angling. One should not
expect to become an expert bait caster overnight; but there are certain fundamentals which, if followed, will not only make for accurate casting, but will enable the beginner to learn quickly. There is
nothing difficult about learning to cast if one remembers that there
is no substitute for correct fundamentals.

POSITION OF REEL

Most beginners make the mistake of casting with the reel on top
of the rod (Plate 1). Instead, one should tip the reel so that it is on
the inside; in other words, the reel is in a vertical position, not a
horizontal one, so that the handle of the reel is pointing straight up
(Plate 2). There are several reasons for this. With the weight on the

lower bearing, the spool can spin more freely and, when the spool is in the vertical position, the wrist can move back and forth with more freedom. If you cast with the left hand, the position will be reversed and the handle of the reel will be pointing straight down.

GRIP

With your rod and reel in the correct position you are ready for the second step, which is the grip. Just as there is a right and a wrong way to grip a tennis racket or a golf club, there is a right and wrong way to grip a rod and reel; but while there may be several methods of gripping a tennis racket or a golf club, there is really only one recognized way of gripping the casting rod. To get the right grip, take the rod and reel in your left hand, grasping the rod at a point of balance just above the reel. Keep in mind that the handle of the reel points

Plate 1. Wrong Position for Overhead Cast

straight up. Place your right hand, palm down, on the handle of the rod. Your index finger will grip the finger trigger of the rod firmly. Your thumb will rest lightly on the spool. Your other three fingers will press the handle of the rod into the palm of your hand. When you have assumed this grip, you will naturally remove your left hand from the rod.

The offset handle and finger trigger grip have come about during the last few years. Some time ago the straight handle was used almost exclusively on casting rods. The new handle with the finger trigger enables you to get a better grip on the handle of the rod and to use your wrist in making the cast.

Your grip should be firm, but not so rigid or tight as to hamper free movement of your wrist. Your three fingers against your palm will exert the greatest pressure. This is necessary in order to give your thumb the proper relaxation and freedom for the important thumbing of the reel. You should feel that you have complete control of the rod and reel (Plate 2 gives the correct grip). Note that the reel handles are straight up, the fingers press the rod into the palm of the hand, and the thumb rests on the flange of the spool.

THUMBING

Proper thumbing of the reel comes with practice. It is a very important fundamental and one that requires much attention. Thumbing is intended to control the speed of the spool; by regulating the pressure of the thumb you are able to control the distance of the cast. If the pressure of your thumb on the reel is too heavy, the bait will be cast only a few yards and, if the pressure is released completely, the result will be a "back-lash." The "back-lash" is caused by the line's running from the reel faster than the weight of the plug can carry it out.

In learning to thumb the spool of the reel you may rest your thumb on the line altogether or you may rest it partially on the line and partially on the flange of the spool. Beginners should try the second method of thumbing the reel; that is, let your thumb rest partially on the line and partially on the flange at the same time. As you practice you should begin to thumb only the flange.

As the rod is moved back for the cast, your thumb should apply a firm pressure in order to allow the weight of the bait to carry the tip of the rod back; this helps give power for the forward cast. The moment the rod begins the forward movement your thumb eases the pressure but remains in contact with the flange and line during the entire cast. Just before the bait hits the target or water your thumb increases the pressure and stops the reel.

Although your thumb is in contact with the spool throughout the entire cast—an important point to remember—continued practice

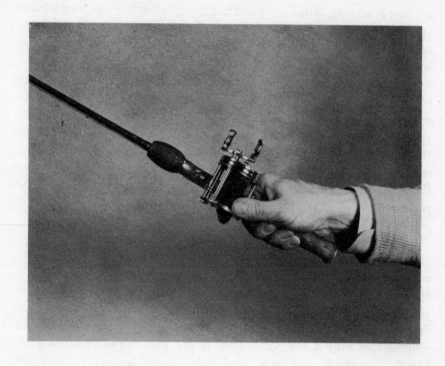

Plate 2. Correct Position for Overhead Cast

will teach you when to release and when to apply proper pressure. The novice will soon learn this technique. Do not be discouraged by a few back-lashes; even the most experienced fisherman will get them occasionally (Plate 2 shows the correct thumb position).

WRIST ACTION

Wrist action cannot be too strongly emphasized. It is important in golf, tennis, or badminton, and doubly important in bait casting.

Before attempting movement of the wrist, check the position of the reel, the grip, and the thumb. Now place a handkerchief or small book under your right arm and you will be forced to rely upon the wrist and forearm, rather than upon the usual beginner's sweeping movement of the arm and body, to make the cast. To practice wrist

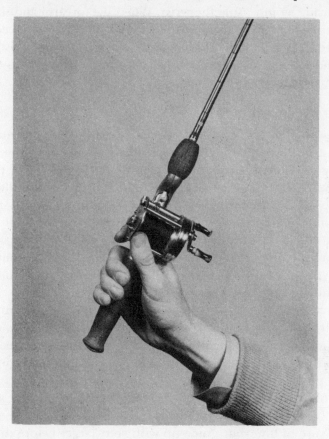

Plate 3. Position of Hand at Top of Cast

action, keep a firm pressure on the flange of the spool and move the rod fairly fast from an almost horizontal position straight up to a vertical position; then, without pausing, bring the rod down in an even faster forward movement. Keep your arm in close to your body and attempt to get all the movement from wrist and forearm. As the rod moves back, the three fingers that press the handle of the rod into the palm of your hand will open (Plate 3). Your fingers should remain in contact with the handle and have control at all

times. As the rod is brought forward your hand is closed. This open-
ing and closing of your hand allows freedom of wrist movement and
gives greater power to the rod tip.

To some beginners it might seem that wrist action alone would
not give sufficient distance to the cast. However, a cast of 100 feet
can be made by just using the wrist. When the forearm and shoulder
are used too much in making the cast, accuracy is sacrificed. It is
therefore important that the beginner concentrate on wrist movement and attempt, as far as possible, to give the impulse to the rod
through proper wrist movement.

THE OVERHEAD CAST

Before you attempt your first cast, check on the fundamentals that
have just been discussed: the reel is on the inside with the handle
pointing straight up, index finger grips the finger trigger of the rod,
thumb rests firmly on the reel flange of the spool, and the other three
fingers press the handle of the rod into the palm of your hand.

Although there are several ways of casting, the overhead cast is
the best one for the beginner to concentrate on. It is the hardest to
learn, but the principles involved in the overhead cast are important
in all types of casting. It is much better to learn the overhead cast
before attempting any other.

To make the cast, stand with your right foot slightly in advance of
your left, with your body facing the target at which you are casting.
This position may be slightly changed to suit the individual. Line
your rod up with the target at which you are aiming, sighting by
the first guide of your rod, that is, the first guide up the rod from the
reel. Hold your rod in such a way that the guide you are sighting
by will be directly in the middle of the target at which you are casting. Be sure to line your guide up with your target before each cast.
Don't forget the handkerchief under your arm to remind you to keep
your elbow in close to your body. Now draw your bait up to about
three or four inches from the end of the rod. From this position you
are ready for your first cast.

With a firm thumb pressure on the spool flange, bring the rod
straight up and back. The backward movement of the rod will open
your hand. When the rod passes a perpendicular position, the tip
of the rod will begin to bend from the weight of the plug. *While the
tip is still bending,* close your fingers into your palm and snap your
wrist forward simultaneously, bringing the rod directly down before

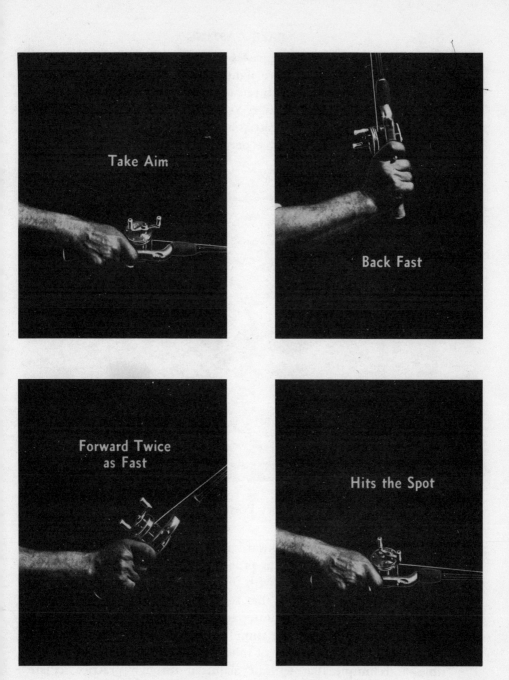

Plate 4. Wrist Movement in Overhead Cast

your eyes. Make sure the rod passes down through the identical position it was in when you were sighting on the target. As the rod is snapped forward, your thumb releases the firm pressure but remains in contact with the spool flange. You should think of the backward movement and the forward cast as a continuous motion. There is no pause when the rod reaches the perpendicular position. If the rod is

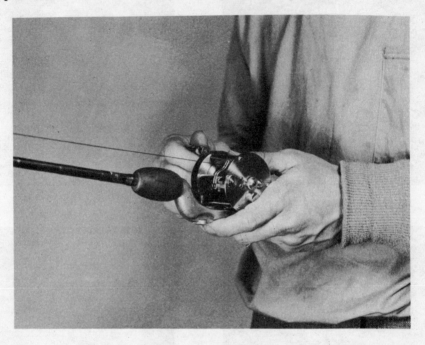

Plate 5. Correct Position for Reeling in

allowed to stop in the backward movement, the rod will lose its spring and lack the power to propel the bait. If the rod has been brought up directly in line with the eye and target and moved forward in the same plane, all that remains to be done is to drop the plug on the target or in the water at the proper distance. Just before the plug hits the target, your thumb increases the pressure and stops the reel. Distance is a matter of releasing the reel spool at the proper time—a technique that will be acquired through practice (Plate 4 shows the overhead cast).

With your eye follow your plug while it is in the air, keeping the rod, reel, and line in alignment. When the plug hits the target or water, shift the rod to your left hand. Hold the reel with the left hand, grasping its handle with the right hand, and then begin to reel in the line (Plate 5). The shifting of the rod to the left hand at the instant the plug hits the spot aimed for is very important and

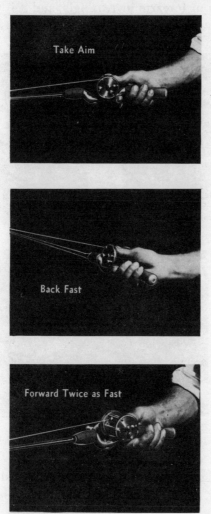

Plate 6. Wrist Movement in Side Cast

will pay dividends in the number of fish caught. After a while you will be able to change hands so fast you will have the plug moving when it strikes the water.

The desire to make long casts tempts the beginner. When he tries this he usually takes his thumb from the spool and invariably gets a back-lash. Thirty-five to fifty feet is the right distance for beginning casts. Do not try to empty your spool of all the line. When you increase distance, you sacrifice accuracy. With your longer casts, you bring into play your forearm increasingly, and it is very essential that good form be practiced in this. For the time being, the beginner

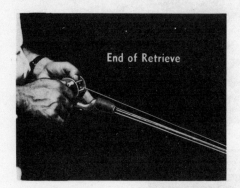

Plate 7. **Wrist Movement** in Flip Cast

should concentrate on good wrist movement and be content with shorter distances. With the shorter casts, you will cover more territory in fishing and also be able to make more casts. If you are content to make accurate casts of forty to sixty feet, you will be rewarded by the number of fish you catch.

The beginner should not do all his casting from a standing position because much of his fishing will be done from a small boat or a canoe. For this reason it is a good idea for the beginner to learn to cast from a sitting position on a small chair or bench. You will be glad that you have mastered the overhead cast when fishing from a sitting position, particularly when there are two or three companions in the boat with you.

THE SIDE CAST

In the side cast the rod is brought back to the right side with the rod parallel to the surface of the water (Plate 6 shows the position of the reel and wrist action of the side cast). The grip is identical with that of the overhead cast except that the reel is on

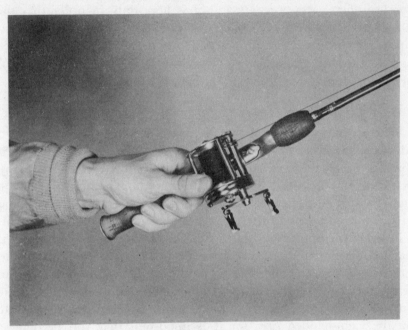

Plate 8. The Left-Handed Cast

top of the rod. The side cast, or "side swipe" as it is called, is largely the result of a wrist and forearm movement. Some will find it to their advantage to keep a firm thumb pressure on the line in making the side cast. The side cast is not very acccurate, but one can get plenty of wrist and arm motion in it and plenty of distance, if there is any advantage in making long casts.

The side cast should never be used when more than one person is fishing from a boat. It should only be used when overhanging branches make it impossible to use the overhead cast. Beginners should refrain from using it at all until the overhead cast has been completely mastered. Many fishermen refuse to be in the same boat with a side-caster, and it is certainly no fun to fish with a person who throws a plug near your head with each cast.

THE FLIP CAST

The flip cast is usually made with the rod in the left hand and results solely from an underhand wrist movement. The flip cast is not a distance cast; its advantage lies in allowing the fisherman to make short casts without wasting time. This cast is not recommended for beginners. Mention is made of it here only in order that the novice may be able to recognize such a cast. This cast requires a fast-tip-action rod; it should be practiced on land before it is used as a means of fishing (Plate 12-13-14 shows the grip and wrist movement of the flip cast).

THE LEFT-HANDED CAST

The technique involved in a left-handed cast overhead is almost identical with that of the right-handed cast. The only difference is that the reel handle is reversed and now points down (Plate 15). Naturally the left-handed cast has an important advantage over the right-handed one: the left-handed cast does not require the changing of the rod and reel to the other hand before reeling in the bait. There is little doubt that the right-handed cast is easier for a right-handed person to learn; but if the beginner has an opportunity to practice during winter months, it would be an advantage for him to learn to cast with either hand. If you are limited, however, as to the amount of time you can expend in practice, by all means concentrate on the right-handed cast, for it is important that you become as accurate as possible.

CHAPTER II

THE BEGINNER'S EQUIPMENT

OFTEN THE BEGINNING fisherman is confronted with the problem of selecting equipment with little idea of what he wants, what he needs, and just how much he should invest in his fishing equipment. The novice should do more than go to a tackle store and ask to be fitted for a fishing trip. If he is going to have real fishing pleasure, he should observe a few guiding principles that will enable him to make the right choice.

The bait caster's equipment consists of a rod, reel, line, various kinds of bait, and other accessories. The beginner must understand that there does not exist an all-round fishing outfit, that is, one set of fishing equipment that is suitable for all kinds of fishing. The equipment described in the following pages applies, for the most part, to bait casting.

Most beginners make the mistake of buying cheap equipment. That statement is not meant to imply that fishing equipment is expensive. You can spend fifty dollars for a single part of your outfit, or you can completely furnish yourself for half that amount. Do not be too extravagant, but do not make the mistake of purchasing equipment you cannot easily cast with or you will deprive yourself of a good deal of fishing pleasure. Be sure that your equipment is properly balanced; then you can look forward to real fishing enjoyment.

The novice should select a rod that has good tip action. It should be between five and six feet long—preferably five to five and one-half feet. With a fast tip action rod, the wrist and forearm action will result in distance and accuracy. A short, stiff rod will not permit enough spring power to be developed by the wrist alone, which means that the novice will be required to use a throwing motion in order to cast his bait. A short, stiff rod is ideal for trolling but not for bait casting.

It is suggested that the beginner select a quadruple, multiplying reel with a fast aluminum spool. The reel should have a level-winding mechanism. The tournament caster uses a reel without the level-winding device. The beginner, however, should have it on his reel. Most people are attracted by a spool that will spin a long time. However, you must have a spool that starts easily and stops quickly. Do not select a reel just because it has a heavy spool and spins longer. The advantages of an aluminum spool reel are quickly demonstrated in actual casting. The light spool gets away to a flying start with little casting effort, and it seldom overruns at the finish.

A smooth and easy-casting small diameter line is recommended. The line should be between ten and fourteen pound test. This test line is much easier to cast with than a heavier one, and with the light line you can land most of the heavy fish if you are careful. Many bait casters make the mistake of selecting a line that has a test of twenty to twenty-five pounds. This test line not only increases back-lashes and makes casting more difficult, but takes away much of the sport of fishing. The large diameter line increases friction in the guides of your rod. Select a good silk or Nylon line that doesn't soak up in the water, for a soggy line makes casting difficult.

THE ROD

The most popular rods today are manufactured of three materials: split bamboo, solid steel, and seamless tapered tubular steel.

A good split bamboo rod has everything a bait caster could expect. It will not stand the strain that the solid steel or tubular steel rod will, but for fineness of action, strength, and sensitivity it is un-equalled. The bamboo rod is especially recommended for the fisher-man who uses light lures in casting. As was stated, bamboo is not as strong as steel, *and will take a set under undue strain.* For that reason, the beginner would be wise to select one of the other kinds of rod. When you have acquired the technique of casting properly and have served your apprenticeship as a fisherman, you will want to own a split bamboo rod.

The solid steel rod lacks the resiliency of bamboo but is extremely strong and powerful. It is a practical one-piece rod and one that will stand a lot of rough treatment. The beginner will make no mistake in selecting this type of rod. It should be of the best grade steel and possess good tip action. Even though they will stand rough treatment, one must be careful with solid steel rods, for the best of them will break.

By far the most popular bait casting rod is the seamless tapered tubular steel rod. The tubular steel rod more nearly approximates the bamboo in action and, for all-round fishing, is probably the best rod to buy. The tubular steel rod not only possesses the strength and action of bamboo, but requires much less care. If you select a seamless tapered tubular steel rod of one-piece design, about five feet or slightly more in length, you will have a serviceable rod that will stand up under the most adverse fishing conditions and, moreover, you will have excellent equipment with which to learn to cast bait.

ROD CONSTRUCTION

Whatever kind of rod you select, you must keep several things in mind with regard to construction and material.

A locking reel seat is necessary. There has been much welcome improvement recently with regard to this part of the rod. Every fisherman will appreciate this safety factor.

Most of the rods today are built with the double grip. They are very comfortable, and they give you a better hold on the rod when you reel in. The off-set handle has proved very popular, but the kind you select will be a matter of your preference. The majority of the grips are covered with cork, which is much preferred to any other kind of material.

To get the best results from the line, the rod must have a good set of guides. Many of them are made of agate or agatine, which is an imitation glass. Some of the best guides are made of metal, especially of mildarbide. It is next to the diamond in hardness and is undoubtedly the best guide to have on your rod. With a good set of guides there is less friction. If the metal is soft or if there is a chip in the agate, the line, of course, will wear quickly.

STYLES

The one-piece rod is the ideal casting rod. It is not weakened at any point by ferrules, although it is a bit unhandy because of its length. But this is more than compensated for by other features.

The beginner who is interested in developing bait casting to a point of perfection will want to use a rod of one-piece design.

The majority of rods in use today are of two or three piece construction. They, of course, do not have the same action or strength as the one-piece rod, but if they are made of the right quality, they serve excellently. Rods of this type are easy to carry and, for this reason, have an advantage over the one-piece rod.

The bait caster must use his own judgment in selecting the style of his rod. All things considered, it would seem that a rod of one-piece design is the best.

LENGTH AND WEIGHT

Rods can be purchased in almost any length desired, but the majority of them range from four and one-half to six and one-half feet. The greatest number of them are around five or five and one-half feet. Length is a matter of personal taste, but a rod of five feet or slightly over with good tip action is the best rod for bait casting.

Most of the rods not only come in different lengths but in different weights as well. The bamboo and the tubular steel types are approximately the same weight, solid steel being slightly heavier. A good casting rod will weigh approximately five ounces, steel an ounce or two more.

CARE OF ROD

The bamboo rod requires a great deal of care. It should be varnished occasionally; that, however, does not mean two or three times each season. If you do much casting, you will want to give your rod a thorough check-up before the season and a few times during the season. If you have never had occasion to varnish your rod, it will be best to secure the help of one who understands the care of rods—better yet, take it to a tackle shop. Care should be taken to see that the windings on the rod do not become loose; again, it is best that the work be done by one who has had experience in the care of bamboo rods.

After the rod has been used, it should be wiped dry before it is put away. Do not put it in a warm room or in a room where there are frequent changes in temperature. A cool closet is the best place for a bamboo rod.

Don't leave the rod on the ground where it might be broken. Do not stand it in the corner and then leave it. The best place to keep the rod is in the case; then you can be sure that nothing will happen to spoil your fishing trip.

The ferrules will cause a great deal of trouble if they become stuck. Be careful in pulling them apart or you will damage the rod. If they are too tight, take them to a tackle shop and have an expert make the adjustment rather than try to file them yourself.

A good bamboo rod, to give the best service, must be taken care of; you cannot handle it as you would a steel rod. Undue strain in fishing can damage your rod to such an extent that it will give only half the service that it might otherwise.

One of the reasons why the steel rod has become so popular is that it requires little care. To prevent rust the steel rod should be wiped dry before it is put away. Many of the steel rods are finished in baked enamel, but they should be wiped nevertheless. It is well to wipe lightly with oil; if the rod is of two or three piece design, a drop of oil on the ferrules will keep them in order.

Even though the rod is made of steel, it can be broken. Many beginners get the idea that it is impossible to break a steel rod. It is true that they are more durable and will stand rougher treatment than bamboo; but to give the best service they must be given proper attention.

THE REEL

In selecting the reel, one must realize that it is by far the most important part of the bait caster's outfit. One can have a stiff rod and heavy line and still manage to make a cast providing he has a good reel. Reels may be purchased with various actions, but the best for bait casting is the quadruple multiplier. This means simply that the spool of the reel revolves four times to every revolution of the handle and enables one to retrieve the line with the least amount of work.

THE LEVEL-WINDER

The beginning bait caster should select a quadruple multiplier with a level-winding mechanism. This mechanism moves back and forth and lays the line evenly on the spool as the handle is turned. A frequent cause of back-lashes is unevenly spooled lines; because it prevents this annoyance, the level-winder is almost a necessity.

A reel with a light spool and a cork arbor will give the best results.

A light aluminum spool will start quickly and is not likely to over-run at the end of the cast. Another common cause of back-lashes is the over-running of a heavy spool at the end of the cast. Do not be fooled into preferring a reel simply because it spins a long time; if you do, you are apt to have trouble with your casting.

Naturally, the kind of material that goes into the reel will have much to do with its efficient operation. Many reels are made today from German silver which is perhaps the best material for the reel. Most reels, however, are made of brass, with either nickle or chrome plating. Stainless steel is excellent material for reel construction because it is non-corrosive. Fishing tackle manufacturers have left nothing undone to achieve mechanical precision in reels. High quality reels are fitted with jewelled bearings. These reels are so well constructed that, if cared for properly, many of them will give a lifetime of service.

Most reels are supplied with a click. This is a device meant to keep the spool from spinning when the spool is not in use. It is very handy, especially in trolling. Many beginners who have not learned to thumb the reel make the mistake of casting with the click on. The click is not placed on the reel for this purpose; casting with the click on will damage the reel.

The reel can be had in various sizes; for practical casting a spool that will hold between 80 and 100 yards of line is sufficient. It is seldom, if ever, that one will make a cast of 100 yards, and, for best all-around casting, a spool holding 60 to 80 yards of line will suffice. A cork arbor on the spool makes it unnecessary to add filler line.

THE "ANTI-BACK-LASH" OR "NO THUMB" REEL

A very popular reel is the "Anti-Back-Lash" or the "No Thumb" reel. The anti-back-lash reel differs from the level-winder very little: the main difference is that the spool is made with over-size axle bearings and the inertia of the spool is proportionate to the radius of the axle spindle. With the large bearings, the spool turns with more friction and less momentum, but it will not over-run and produce a back-lash.

One would naturally expect to get more distance with the level-winder, and this is true. The inexperienced caster, however, who uses the anti-back-lash reel will average just as much distance as the novice who uses a level-winder for the simple reason that the former does not waste his time untangling back-lashes. This would not be true of the experienced caster. The beginner will not go wrong in learning to cast with an anti-back-lash reel. He can learn to thumb the spool regardless of the anti-back-lash mechanism, and he can emphasize wrist action. The beginner should use this reel only long enough to learn the correct form in casting; otherwise the fundamentals of thumbing the spool properly will be somewhat neglected.

The big advantage of the anti-back-lash reel is that it enables you to make a perfect cast the first time you try. For the man who fishes only a few days each season and does not have a chance to practice bait casting, it makes a very good reel. It is no fun wasting half one's time undoing a nasty back-lash. The anti-back-lash reel makes night fishing more enjoyable, for it is difficult to prevent back-lashes when you are casting at night with a level-winder, but this problem is solved by the anti-back-lash reel.

There are several other styles of reels which the beginner will learn more about as he becomes interested in the sport of bait casting. The tournament reel, for example, is somewhat different from the level-winder or the anti-back-lash, but, for all practical purposes, the last two will serve the beginner.

CARE OF THE REEL

To obtain the service and pleasure that the reel is meant to give requires a certain amount of care. Nothing will wreck a reel quicker than sand or dirt. Do not leave your reel on the ground, and do not keep it in a place where dust might get into it. When you are not using the reel, keep it in a small pouch where dust and dirt cannot get at it.

Many excellent reels have been ruined by curiosity. The beginner should be careful in taking his reel apart. Unless you are acquainted with the mechanism, you had best get help from someone who understands the working of reels. It is not often that the reel needs to be taken apart, but when it is necessary, there are several things to keep in mind.

Clean all the working parts with benzine or gasoline. It is best to use a brush in cleaning the reel, since a rag might leave lint. A chamois serves the purpose very well. After the reel has been thoroughly cleaned out, put a drop of good oil in each end of the spool bushing, line carriage, and crank shaft. Be sure that a high grade reel oil is used, and guard against putting too much oil on the reel. Too much oil will tend to spoil the action of the reel and will do

more damage than too little oil. On the gears use a good grease—
mutton tallow or vaseline is recommended. If your reel is made of
corrosive material and you use it for salt water fishing, be sure to
wash it thoroughly when you have finished your day's fishing.

When you reassemble the reel, be sure that every screw is properly
tightened. Be careful to use the right tool in working on the reel,
and keep in mind that your reel is a delicate instrument designed to
give the best service only if these few simple rules are observed:

1. Exercise care in taking the reel apart.
2. Be sure to remove all dirt, taking care not to leave dust in the
process of cleaning.
3. Keep the reel well oiled, taking care to use the right oil and
remembering not to over-oil.
4. Be sure that all parts are adjusted and all screws kept tight.
5. Replace worn-out parts at once.

THE LINE

In selecting a line for bait casting, keep in mind that it is almost
as important a part of the fishing equipment as the rod and reel.
Many beginners make the mistake of buying a line with which it is
impossible to cast efficiently.

Be sure that the line is of a small diameter; for best casting pur
poses, it should be soft braided. The soft braid has a tendency to
soak up more water than the hard braid, but, for a combination of
quality and casting pleasure, the soft braid is the best. The hard
braid is more durable, but many bait casters do not enjoy casting
with it. Until recently silk has been the only material suitable for
casting lines. There is now on the market a synthetic fiber called
Nylon that bids fair to become very popular as a fishing line. It has
the casting qualities of silk and, from all indications, appears to be
more durable.

The size of the line is important. Bait casting lines can be had in
almost any size or test desired, but beginners should use a ten to
fourteen pound test line. A heavier test line *can* be used, but for
casting pleasure a line of the above-mentioned size is best. This does
not mean that heavier fish than fourteen pounders cannot be landed
on this test line; actually, it is possible to bring much heavier fish
to the boat and land them with this line if you are skillful. Further-
more, you will find that there is a great deal more sport in using a

light line than in using one that resembles a tow rope. It is accuracy that counts in bait casting, and with a light line you are able to drop your bait in the most likely spots.

Color is a matter of preference. As far as the author has been able to find out, color makes little difference to the fish.

CARE OF THE LINE

If the line is going to give even a small part of its intended service, it must be dried each time it is used. The line will rot if it is allowed to remain on the reel wet. Therefore, after each fishing session, take the line off and dry it in the shade. Such a precaution will be rewarded by a constantly safe line.

Be careful about casting with knots in the line. It often happens in casting that a small knot occurs. The sensible thing to do is to take a few minutes to remove it; if you don't, the test strength of your line will be reduced almost forty per cent.

Check for cuts in the guides. Nothing will wear a line more quickly than casting it through a guide that has been accidently chipped.

Many fishermen make a practice of breaking one or two feet from the end of the line whenever a great deal of rough treatment has worn it, for the wear of the line is much greater at this particular point than elsewhere. Remember, a damaged line may mean the difference between landing the big one and talking about the big one that got away.

Check your line at the end of a day's fishing, especially if you have been casting into reeds or if you have accidentally gotten your bait into a tree or bush. There is a very great possibility that it has been damaged; rather than risk losing a fish, it is a wise policy to change lines.

ADDITIONAL EQUIPMENT

Although the essentials of bait casting—rod, reel, and line—have already been discussed, there are certain other pieces of equipment that the bait caster will find not only helpful but requisite in landing a fish. It is natural that the selection of baits is of primary importance, and an entire chapter will be devoted to this subject. There are, however, a number of useful articles, both directly and indirectly related to the angler's art, which can be classed as necessary equipment. These include: tackle kit, stringer, cleaning knife, pocket knife, extra line, reel oil, weights of different sizes, landing net or a gaff, leaders (wire), pliers, and flashlight.

The tackle kit well deserves its place at the head of the list, for a compact, convenient box which has compartments for the fisher-man's array of equipment, forms the basis of any bait caster's auxil-iary outfit. It should be noted here too that one's financial means, as well as his preference regarding tackle he likes to carry along on trips, should be his guide when he selects, not only his rod and reel, but his kit as well. There is, of course, the danger of having too large a stock of equipment as well as the danger of having too small a kit. The outfit, however, should be simple. With simplicity as his slogan, the bait caster should encounter little difficulty in assembling an inexpensive, efficient, and wholly satisfactory tackle box.

Another important piece of equipment is the stringer. There are various stringers on the market made of chain, cord, or rope,— ranging from the very expensive to the very cheap. Many of them have hooks, either swivel or snap, but the one that seems most suited to the beginning bait caster is a moderately priced rope stringer, about six feet long, with one swivel and several snap hooks. These snap hooks are detachable; extra ones can be bought that can quickly be put into place. Almost all stringers are equipped with a sharp needle point, and this needle is rather important.

A cleaning knife and an all-purpose pocket knife should be in-cluded, for they will certainly prove their worth before the bait caster's day is over. The pocket knife has a number of uses, and the cleaning knife is essential for efficient cleaning of your catch.

Casting weights of various sizes and types should be included, be-cause you must suit the depth that your lures are to sink to the fishing conditions. Fishing, as has already been stressed, is a sport which requires adaptability to many uncertainties. A good assort-ment of weights would include a few plain ringed sinkers for still fishing, several swiveled dipsey sinkers to be used with spinners and light lures, and some snap swivel sinkers. Weights ought to range from the very heavy to the very light.

The landing net or the gaff, although it may not fit the tackle box as conveniently as some other equipment, is nevertheless quite important. A few fish may be safely landed with the hands, but the muskie, pickerel, pike, and several others have sharp teeth that can-not be disregarded. Although the gaff is used by many experts, the net is suggested for the beginning bait caster. A good-sized net will be found valuable for use in a boat, i.e., one with a frame of sixteen or eighteen inch diameter, with a good strong net. The frames are usually collapsible and have a two-piece handle. The importance of a strong frame and handle cannot be under-emphasized. Most frames are sold without the net; nets come in a number of types— standard linen, brown waterproof cord, and waterproof braided linen.

The beginner often makes the mistake of not including several wire leaders in his tackle box. The leader makes it easier to change baits, as well as easier to eliminate the possibility of the fish cutting or fraying the line with his sharp teeth. Gut leaders are rather in-effective because they can be cut, but wire leaders are very efficient, although they are sometimes stiff and prevent easy movement of the bait. Choose, therefore, a wire leader that is flexible. Leaders of picture cord are good, made with a loop at one end and a swivel snap at the other. An assortment of leaders, ranging in size from the six inch ones for bass or wall-eyes to the eight and ten inch ones for Great Northern and muskie, should be a part of every outfit. The wire leader must not be drawn through the guides, for there is a possibility of cracking a guide, which is very liable to result in cutting the line.

Two of the indispensables of every tackle box are a pair of pliers and a flashlight. These two articles will come in handy always, and they take up little space in the tackle box. A few other suggestions for your box are: a small first-aid kit, various sizes of hooks, oil for the reel, extra line, odds and ends of wire, a bit of wrapping silk, and a small pair of scissors if you have a bamboo rod. Finally, choose your outfit carefully; without proper equipment neither expert nor beginner can enjoy successful fishing.

CHAPTER III

TIPS ON FISHING

As a rule, most fishermen are very generous and willing when it comes to giving advice about angling. It is typical of the people who fish that they should help the beginner; often he is given advice whether he solicits it or not. However, the beginner must understand that much of such information is either very general or affecting only one specific situation. If this were not so, and if there were cut and dried rules that applied to *all* fishing, a great deal of the sporting element would be lost. There are, however, a few tips that the beginning bait caster can profit by, and they will help make his first fishing experiences more profitable.

Here are a few hints on how to cast the bait: make up your mind that you are going to cast overhead and that the only time you are going to cast differently is when it is impossible to place your bait where you want it with an overhead cast. Remember that the side cast is not as accurate as the overhead and that your companion deserves to be considered.

Bait casting is largely a matter of accuracy. It isn't the long distance caster who brings in the most fish, but the fellow who is able to place his bait where he wants it. Too often the beginner makes the mistake of trying to throw the bait as far as possible, when a short, easy flick of the wrist would send his bait fifty or sixty feet and result in a strike. It is, of course, true that you are trying to catch fish, and yet a great deal of pleasure can be derived merely from being able to place your bait within a few inches of a lily pad or an old dead log. Keep in mind that when you increase distance you increase the possibility of a back-lash. It is better to make a dozen short, accurate casts than to make a half dozen long ones and spend most of your time undoing a back-lash.

WHEN AND WHERE

The beginning bait caster must keep an open mind at all times, especially in regard to the time and place for casting. There is a "consistency of disagreement" in these matters. There are experienced fishermen who believe fish will not bite in the rain, or when there is an east wind, or when the moon changes, or during a thunder storm. The truth is that fish can be caught under almost any circumstances on certain occasions. It is difficult to establish iron-clad rules about attracting fish. Study the feeding habits of the different fish, and, gradually, from your own experience, you will learn the best time to fish for bass, wall-eye, and other fresh water fish. Be willing to accept suggestions, but do not be afraid to experiment yourself.

For the most part, bait casting is more successful near the shore, around logs, weeds, lily pads, and other such growth. This is where the fish feed, so you should expect to do most of your casting along the shore. If you happen to be on a lake, be sure to try the inlet or outlet. Be sure, also, to try the sand bars for wall-eyes and small mouth bass. Remember the most likely spots and, if you are not successful, come back and try again. Many fishermen do all their casting in toward the shore. This is a good method of fishing, but you only fish a small area when you cast in that direction. Try casting parallel to the shore, for, by doing this, you have your bait in "fishing" territory from the time your bait enters the water until you pick it up for another cast.

RETRIEVING THE BAIT

A common fault of many beginners is the improper position of the left hand in holding the rod and reel when retrieving the bait. The correct position is shown in Plate 8. You will note that the left hand grasps the reel so that it is in the palm of the left hand. In this position, the hand has a secure grip on the reel and rod as well. The hand is also ready for quick action in setting the hooks when the fish strikes. Some anglers grasp the rod just in front of the reel in order to drain off the excess water and to put tension on the line. The water, however, produces enough tension on the line, and the thumb alone can be used to drain off the water.

Another common fault of the bait caster is to retrieve his bait too quickly. The tournament caster or the "dry land fisherman" often gets into the habit of fast casting, paying little attention to the manner in which he "works" his bait. If you are casting a surface plug, let it rest for a second and then begin your retrieve. A frequent jerk or change of pace will often result in a strike.

The bait caster who consistently brings home a good catch has usually learned to make his bait appear to be a wounded minnow, a floundering frog, or some other natural fish food. The natural inclination of fish is to feed on one another. Make your bait act alive.

HOOKING AND LANDING

When you get a strike, be sure to set your hooks. This is done by thumbing the reel firmly, and then, with a fast flick of the wrist, tipping the rod up. Do not hesitate, or the "big one" might escape from your bait. It is not necessary to jerk with all your strength; you might tear the bait from the mouth of the fish or break the line. Just set the hooks with a quick and firm movement. Some anglers retrieve their bait with the rod pointing straight to the heavens. This is not a good position, for it is then difficult to set the hooks, and many a fish has been lost because the hooks were not properly set. Retrieve the bait with your rod tilted slightly above parallel to the water.

When you have set your hooks, immediately tilt your rod down again. By doing this, you relieve your line of the strain and let your fishing equipment play the fish. If he wants to fight, be careful that you do not strain the rod; give him line, but make sure there is no slack in it at any time. When you get your fish up near the boat and find he is still fighting, move him around in a figure eight in the water to tire him out. Don't be fooled into thinking there is no fight left in your catch if he seems to give up just as you are about to land him. Keep your fish away from under the boat, and don't get tangled up in the oars. Some experts recommend moving in toward the shore and pulling the "big ones" on land, but you always take the chance of losing your catch when you do this.

In landing a fish, do not lift him out with the rod. This not only strains the rod, but it is also a very good way to lose a fish. It is best to use a net or a gaff. In using a landing net, be sure to lead the fish over the submerged net; don't try to scoop it under the fish.

Sooner or later, the beginner will want to acquire the technique of gaffing the large fish in the hopes that some day the experience can be used. Gaffing is done with one quick motion, hooking the fish from below well back toward the tail. Fish without teeth can be lifted by taking hold of their mouths, but this is not recommended for the beginner since the chance of getting a barb in the hand is very great. Some anglers place their fingers in the eyes of the fish and lift the fish out; but this is not a very pleasant technique, especially for the beginner. It is, however, very effective.

Very often you will hook a fish too small to keep. If you lift the fish out with your hands, be sure to wet them before you handle the fish or you will injure him. With your wet hands you are apt to squeeze the fish in order to hold him. You must, however, do this very lightly, or you are liable to do more harm than if you had lifted the fish with dry hands.

NIGHT BAIT CASTING

The beginning bait caster will soon learn that most game fish can be caught at night. This is especially true of bass and wall-eyed pike. You will find that, quite often, your largest fish may be caught after the sun goes down.

If possible, use an anti-back-lash reel for your night casting. It is indeed exasperating to have to untangle a back-lash at night, especially when your flashlight is back on shore.

Know the territory you are fishing at night. You should be well acquainted with the shore and have a very good idea of logs, thick vegetation, and low hanging branches.

Experience will teach you the best kind of bait to use for night fishing. You should take along several surface bait (luminous ones are good), several weedless lures, pork rind on a spinner, and several kinds of natural bait. Your choice of bait will depend a great deal upon the water and section of country in which you are fishing.

Black baits are often effective at night. When you consider the fact that a fish-eye's view of a bait outlines a dark bait against a light sky, you can understand why a fish will strike a dark bait on a light night.

WEIGHT OF BAIT

Most of the wooden lures and a good many of the metal ones weigh $5/8$ ounce, which seem to be the best weight for bait casting.

Bait, of course, are manufactured in various weights, ranging from ¼ ounce to an ounce; naturally, the heavier baits are easier to cast.

There has been a tendency recently to increase the use of light bait. Everyone, regardless of how expert he is, has difficulty in changing from a heavy bait to a light one. The easiest way to compensate for this change of weight in baits is to increase the length of line-lead from the tip of the rod to the bait. The usual distance of line-lead for a ⅝ ounce or heavier bait is between four to six inches, although some fishermen use two or three inches. If you are using a wire leader four to six inches long, you will be all right. When you change to lighter baits, increase this line-lead, and after several casts you yourself can tell what the proper distance should be. By increasing the length of lead-line, you increase the casting arc of the bait; a longer line-lead allows you to cast a light bait with the same amount of wrist action or effort you were using in casting the ⅝ ounce one.

HOOKS

The number of hooks you use on your bait will be a matter of personal preference. Several years ago treble-hooked baits were the most popular, and they are still used a great deal today. However, the double-hook and single-hook baits have become popular recently for the very simple reason that they are equally as efficient in catching fish as the treble-hooked baits. Some fishermen use only a single hook and look down on their brethren who use treble-hooked baits. There seems to be an element of fair play involved in the question, and it is likely that the beginning bait caster will enjoy his fishing more if the spirit of sportsmanship be included in the tackle box.

TACKLE KNOTS

Every angler should know how to tie at least two or three different knots. In bait casting, a lot of time is saved by tying a loop on the end of the line. After you have tied the loop, slip it through the eye of the swivel on the lure, pass it over the lure, and pull it up. This is a much stronger connection than a simple knot, and it will not slip (Diagram 1 shows some favorite knots of the fisherman).

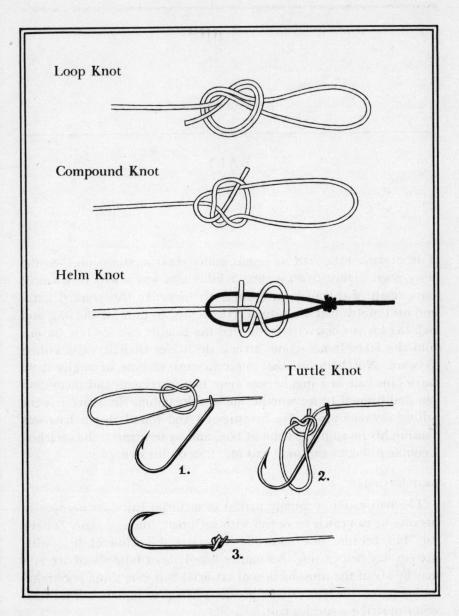

Loop Knot

Compound Knot

Helm Knot

Turtle Knot

1.

2.

3.

Diag. 1. Useful Fishermen's Knots

CHAPTER IV

BAIT

THE CASTING PLUG had its origin under these circumstances—so the story goes: "Once upon a time a fisherman was seated in his boat on a small Michigan lake, cussing his luck. He had worked hard, and his rewards had been small. He decided to quit for the day, and lighting his last cigarette, he hurled the gaudily colored box far out into the lake. It no sooner struck the water than it went sailing skyward. Not being of the comic newspaper type of angler, who carries his bait in a jug, he was more than surprised, and thereupon pinched himself to see whether he was dreaming. No, there it went sailing skyward again. He investigated and found that a bass was venting his rage on the colored box, and so securing it, he attached a couple of hooks and soon had Mr. Bass on his string." [1]

ARTIFICIAL BAIT

The bait caster is usually partial to artificial bait—not necessarily because he can catch more fish with such bait (though many believe so), but because one naturally associates this kind of bait with present day bait casting. No matter how true or false the above tale may be about the introduction of artificial bait, one thing is certain: nothing gives the bait caster a greater thrill than to have a fish break water to strike a surface bait.

Some baits are made to catch the fish, while others are made to catch the fisherman, so the beginner must use care in selecting his bait. Remember that fish are to be found in three places: along the

[1] *Practical Bait Casting,* by Larry St. John, by permission of the MacMillan Company, Publishers.

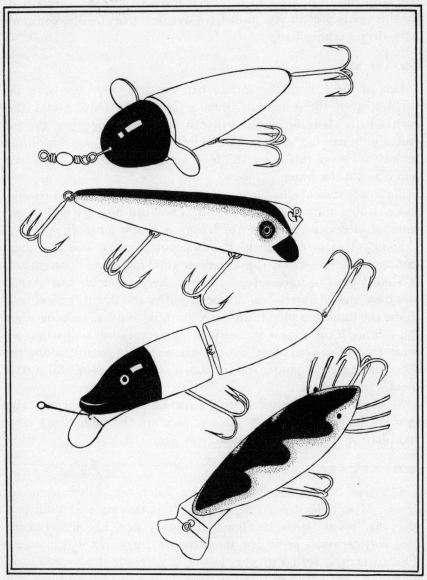

Diag. 2. Surface and Semi-Surface Baits

shore, near the surface, and in deep water. You must select your bait with this in mind. You will need surface and near-surface bait; for the weedy growth you must have weedless bait; finally, you must have deep-running bait.

SURFACE BAIT

One of the reasons the surface bait remains very popular is the thrill it gives the fisherman when a fish breaks water and strikes such a bait. Many fishermen will cast a surface plug when the fish just aren't striking surface bait. The reason they give for this is logical: it's more fun to see 'em hit a surface plug than it is to hook 'em beneath the water.

Surface bait can be had in a variety of colors, but the most popular has a white body with a red head. They can also be had in any number of designs, some of which appear almost fantastic.

Some experts recommend the luminous surface bait for night casting, while others say the luminous glow makes no difference. It is a good plan to have several of them in your tackle box. When you have a good variety, do not be afraid to use them. A good time to use the luminous plug is the early morning and late evening when the fish are feeding near the surface. Sometimes fish will strike another type of surface plug; but fish are generally feeding along the shore during these hours, and, of course, a surface plug will attract them (Diagram 2).

Accuracy is important in casting a surface plug. It is not necessary to make long distance casts. Rather, pick out the most likely spots and place your bait near lily pads, logs, etc.

SEMI-SURFACE BAIT

The semi-surface bait floats on the water but, when retrieved, dives and wobbles from side to side. It is this style of plug that gives the "plunk" noise familiar to the bait caster. The action of the plug will depend a great deal upon the way in which it is handled. The faster it is reeled in, the deeper it goes; for that reason, care must be exercised when using it in shallow water where there is a thick growth on the bottom.

These plugs are made in various designs and almost any color (Diagram 2). The semi-surface plug, because of its action, will attract fish when other bait seem to fail completely. As with the surface plug, the best color combination seems to be red and white, but

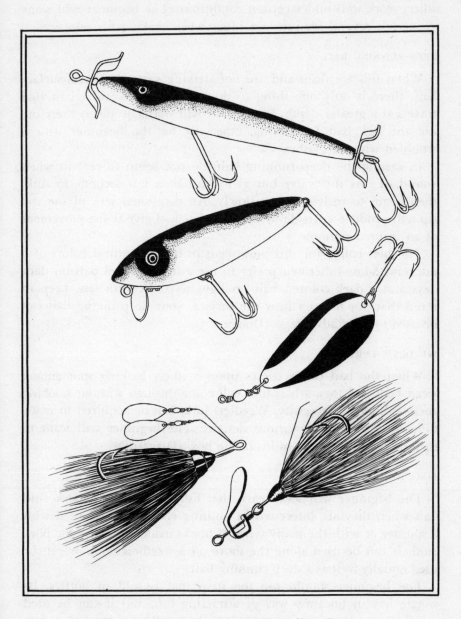

Diag. 3. Underwater and Weedless Lures

others work well under certain conditions. The beginner will want to include several semi-surface plugs when making his selection.

DEEP RUNNING BAIT

When fish are deep and are not striking surface or near-surface bait, there is only one thing to do and that is to use a bait that travels at a greater depth. Such a bait will not float and is therefore not the best bait for casting, especially for the beginner who is troubled with backlashes.

In casting the deep running bait, do not begin to reel in when your bait hits the water but give the bait a few seconds to sink; then begin to reel in rather slowly. An occasional jerk of the rod tip will produce a wiggle in the bait that will give it the movement of an injured minnow.

The best colors for this plug seem to be the natural colors of a minnow. Some fishermen prefer to use a light colored bait on dark days and a dark colored bait on light days. Nevertheless, keep in mind that, for fish not near the surface, your deep diving bait can be used to good advantage (Diagram 3).

WEEDLESS LURES

When the bait caster comes upon a likely looking spot among weed beds and logs, a bait that will come through without hooking them is almost a necessity. Weedless lures can be acquired in many different sizes and in various designs. The beginner will want to include several of these in his tackle box (Diagram 3).

PORK RIND

The beginner will soon learn that fish often strike a pork rind bait when they are interested in nothing else. It can be used with a spinner or with the many types of hooks made especially for pork rind. It can be used along the shore on a weedless hook or can be used equally well as a deep running bait.

The beginner should use the strip that is sold in bottles. Its wiggle has an uncanny way of attracting fish, and it can be used under almost any circumstances. It is the stand-by of the bait caster, attracting fish when everything else fails.

SPINNERS AND SPOONS

The names of these lures are often confusing to the novice. Although in bait casting a great many of the metal revolving lures are called spinners, the spinners designed especially for bait casting are of lighter construction than the spoon. The spoon can be used as a casting bait, although the larger sizes are used mostly for trolling. Both the spoon and spinner are used a great deal by the bait caster and with quite a measure of success (Diagram 3).

In selecting your spoon and spinner baits, be certain that they are of the type that spin freely. It is impossible to recommend a particular kind of the large assortment that is offered on the market; it will suffice to remark that this is a bait you should have.

NATURAL BAIT

There are certain times when fish can be lured successfully only by a natural bait. The beginning bait caster, consequently, will do well to acquaint himself with the various kinds of live bait as well as with the best conditions under which to use them.

The common worm, called by some the angleworm, by others the fishworm, can well take its place at the head of the group of natural baits. The worm has proved successful so many times when other baits—artificial and natural—have failed, that it would seem its recognition should be assured. This is not entirely the case, however, for many bait casters are inclined to look with scorn upon the lowly worm. Although it is uncertain whether the wiggle of the head and tail or the flavor of this fish food attracts the fish, the fact remains that the worm is one of the most popular of baits. The four kinds of worm that are most important for fishing are: the black-headed worm, which is relatively dark colored and found most often in garden soil; the ringed worm, the body of which is ringed and is flatter than the black-headed one and which is found usually under old manure piles; the marsh worm, identified by its light blue color and a white ring, the favorite habitat of which is beneath rocks, decayed leaves, etc.; and the redheaded worm, dark red in color, which is found in rich earth, and which is thicker than the others. Of these, the first, the black-headed worm, is by far the best and commonest bait. Part of the popularity of the worm is due perhaps to the fact that it can be found almost anywhere.

The best method of hooking a worm is to run the hook through the skin about one third of the way down the body; then skip a third and run the hook through again. About a quarter of the length of the worm should be left to wriggle loosely at the barb end of the hook.

Another all-round live bait is the minnow. Contrary to the popular conception that any small fish is a minnow is the fact that the minnow is a distinctly separate fish family which includes some hundred species. Although more minnows are found in warm, slow streams, the liveliest, and therefore the best bait are those minnows taken from swift, cold waters. The choice of the most effective minnow varies naturally with the type of fish sought. For the pike family, a large minnow, eight to ten inches long, seems to be the most popular. Several types of artificial bait can also be used with minnows to make them more attractive. The best method of determining your choice is to try out several baits until the particular minnow that suits the fish's fancy is found. Running the hook through the lower lip and out the nostril is the accepted method of hooking a minnow, although it is better to hook large minnows through both lips (Diagram 4).

The beginning bait caster will find the frog a good natural bait. Medium sized frogs are best and, fortunately, are the easiest to find. They frequent low, marshy meadows and the shallow waters and banks of lakes and streams. Frogs are most effective when used in lake fishing. There are two good methods of hooking the frog (Diagram 4). No better bait can be found for black bass, especially the large-mouth, and for the pike family.

The larvae of the dobson fly, known to fishermen as the helgramite, is a fairly successful bait for bass fishing, but its use for casting is somewhat limited because of its small size. The helgramite can be found under large stones, in the rapids or riffles of a stream, and under damp, rotten wood. Its body is brown and has three pairs of legs extending from it. Its jaws are powerful, and it looks like a vicious insect. The proper manner of hooking a helgramite is to run the hook under the hard collar behind the head, leaving it free to wriggle.

Grasshoppers, crickets, and other insects are all good natural baits and will prove their worth if the fisherman will give them a try.

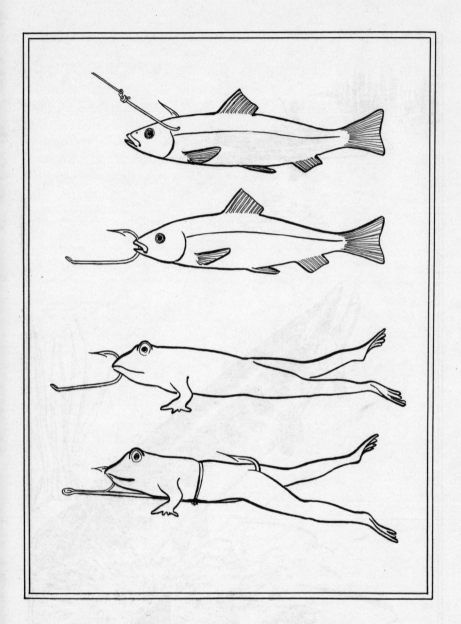

Diag. 4. Methods of Hooking Minnows and Frogs

CHAPTER V

FRESH WATER GAME FISH

IF THE BEGINNING bait caster would make his fishing experiences more enjoyable and more profitable, he would do well to follow up these few pages of information regarding our fresh water game fish with further reading. Although the scientific terminology and ichthyologic standing of fish are unnecessary for the bait caster to learn, he should at least be able to tell what variety of fish he has taken from the water. Nevertheless, the beginner need not feel too sophomoric should he be unable to identify his catch, for there have been hundreds of fishermen, trying their luck for many summers, who are unable to determine, with any accuracy, the variety of fish they catch.

Strangely enough, even many of these experienced fishermen cannot distinguish a small mouth bass from a large mouth, or a walleye from a pickerel. There are many simple, sure marks of distinction that the angler can learn. The confusion may be attributed to several causes: in the first place, a fish that might be going under one name in certain localities is very likely to be called something entirely different a few hundred miles away; secondly, it is a common fallacy to call a great northern pike a pickerel; thirdly, the wall-eyed pike has been associated with the pike family to such an extent that many fishermen do not know that he is really a member of the perch family; and, finally, some anglers refer to the wall-eyed pike as a pickerel. Thus, the following pages have been written in the hope that they will clear up at least some of the misunderstanding that has become prevalent regarding our fresh water game fish.

It has long been common knowledge that the fisherman, in order to catch fish, needs to be smarter than the fish. Fishing under the most ideal conditions is an uncertain proposition; although uncertainty makes the sport fascinating, it means that the bait caster must realize there is more to fishing than the expert handling of a rod. The experienced angler is that rare person who has not only spent many hours of practice learning the art of using a rod and reel, but has studied his fish carefully. It is from his reading and experience that he has been able to gain a practical knowledge of the feeding habits, the likes and dislikes, and the habitat of his intended prey.

THE BLACK BASS

Wherever fishermen gather you will hear tales of that gentleman of fish, the black bass. Perhaps the best known of all the so-called game fish is the bass, because the two species, large-mouth and small-mouth, are native to the fresh waters of almost every lake, stream, and creek of America. Inasmuch as two-thirds of all fishermen are bass fishermen and two-thirds of all the equipment in this country is designed for black bass, it might be well for the beginner to know something of the life, habits, and characteristics of this gamiest of game fishes.

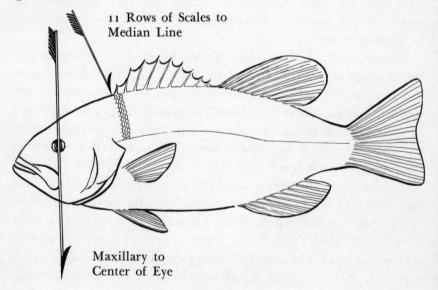

11 Rows of Scales to
Median Line

Maxillary to
Center of Eye

Diag. 5. Small Mouth Black Bass

The black bass, which—paradoxically enough—is not black at all, but ranges, in both varieties, from pale yellow through different shades of green and yellow-bronze to dark, almost black-green, is a member of the sunfish family; the two species are known scientifically as Micropterous Dolomieu, the small-mouth, and Micropterous Salmoides, the large-mouth (Diagram 6).

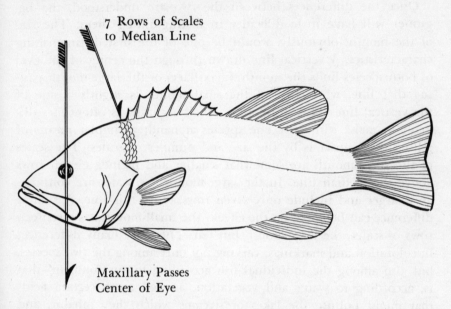

7 Rows of Scales
to Median Line

Maxillary Passes
Center of Eye

Diag. 6. Large Mouth Black Bass

The black bass thrives in practically any kind of water under conditions that other game fish find impossible to live in. In addition to this, he combines many of the characteristics of his less hardy brothers—the speed of the trout and the strength of the salmon—with a fighting ability all his own. He has a plucky sort of courage which gives him a fearlessness in attacking other living objects, often at the risk of his own life. It is this combination of adaptability with unyielding spirit that makes the bass the game fish of the people.

There has long been a controversy among fishermen over the comparative gameness of the two species. The small-mouth, many have asserted, is smaller, faster, and a better leaper, while the large-mouth is a stronger, heavier fish. One thing is certain: both fish are lively. Since the small-mouth is generally taken from fast

waters, the angler must fight not only against the fish, but against
the pull of the water as well. This, naturally, is in favor of the small-
mouth. The large-mouth lives usually in warmer waters, and this
is likely to make him more sluggish than his brother. Nevertheless,
the large-mouth seems to have a greater adaptability and a greater
distribution than the small-mouth.

Once the differences between the two are understood, the beginner will have little difficulty in distinguishing them. The size
of the mouth, obviously, would be one of the first distinguishing
characteristics. A vertical line drawn through the center of the eyes
of both species finds the mouth (maxillary) of the large-mouth pass-
ing that line, while that of the small-mouth is slightly inside of
the vertical line. This distinction, albeit accurate, is oftentimes difficult to make with only one species at hand; a simpler means of
telling them apart is by the size and number of scales. The scales
of the small-mouth are somewhat smaller and include eleven rows
above the median line. In the large-mouth the scales are consider-
ably larger and include only seven rows above this line. A similar
difference can be noted on the cheek: the small-mouth has seventeen
rows of scales, the large-mouth but ten. There are many differences
in coloration and markings, varying not only among the two species,
but also among the individual fish according to environment—that
is, according to water and vegetation, as well as to certain acids
that might pollute the lakes or streams which they inhabit, and
finally according to the age of the fish. The United States Com-
mission on Fish and Fisheries says: "The most reliable characteristic
for distinguishing the large-mouth from the small-mouth bass is
the number of rows of scales on the cheeks. The colors of each
species may vary with age, and the size of the mouth varies with
the size of the fish, but the scales are constant under all conditions."

The eye of the small-mouth may often show a spot of red in the
iris, although this is more often the exception than the rule. There
is, in the large-mouth, a definite "dent" in the forehead, while the
forehead of the small-mouth is always rounded. The small-mouth
has a trimmer body than the large-mouth and a rounder tail.

The black bass differs from the rest of the sunfish family by being
larger, more elongated in form, with an oblong body, conic head,
and jaws in broad villiform bands. The dorsal fin has a deep notch
with low, rather weak spines.

The small-mouth has been called the more aristocratic of .the two, since he thrives in deeper, cooler waters with a gravelly or rocky bottom. The most likely spots to find him in are around rocks and ledges and at the foot of rapids. He feeds upon crawfish and minnows, as well as upon frogs, insects, etc.—the natural food of fish with teeth in the jaws. When young, his chief food consists of minute crustaceans and the larval forms of insects. The teeth of both species are closely packed and practically incapable of wounding, merely serving the purpose of holding the prey securely. The small-mouth can live in ponds, lakes, creeks, or streams having cold bottom springs. Although both the large and small-mouth are frequently found in the same lake, the small-mouth prefers the faster waters.

The large-mouth is less particular, both about the waters he inhabits and the food he eats. He is distributed throughout the South and the North, thereby giving evidence of greater adaptability. He is more often found, however, in warmer waters with weedy bottoms, such as shallow lakes, slow streams, ponds, and places where the small-mouth would eventually lose out. On the other hand, the large-mouth is adaptable to the habitat of the small-mouth. He feeds on much the same things as the small-mouth, the large-mouth being perhaps a little more partial to frogs and warm water minnows.

The average weight of the large-mouth varies from two pounds in the North to as much as four pounds in the South. A prize-winning large-mouth in the northern districts will run to a maximum of perhaps nine pounds, while in the intermediate or southern districts such a catch would attract little attention, since ten and eleven pounders are matters of record there.

The black bass has all five senses: sight, hearing, feeling, smell, and taste; experiments have proved that he has both intelligence and understanding. He shows anger, hatred, and combativeness and, in building his nest, he shows constructive ability.

Fishing is, at best, rather uncertain sport. No matter how much experience or knowledge one possesses, he is never certain, whether expert, beginner, or amateur, to make a good catch. Although the bass so far has seemed to be the "fisherman's ideal fish," he does exhibit what—for want of a better word—can be called temperament. He very often approaches extremes of fickleness, and his moods are often incomprehensible to the angler. There are times when his appetite is seemingly insatiable, when he goes after anything and everything that looks like something to eat; then again he may show no interest whatever in food. Often he may be roused to fits of anger when something is passed across his line of vision. It is just as important to understand this changeable attitude, this inconsistency, as it is to understand the typical actions of the bass. Such fickleness on the part of the fish is indeed a good test of the angler's patience and skill.

The question of hibernation of bass has been discussed a great deal by authorities. Some observers contend that bass do not hibernate except in the northern states. Evidence proves, however, that, while bass in the North may bury themselves in the mud, burrow under sunken logs, under weeds, or even in the crevices of rocks, bass in the South likewise have a season wherein they go into a seclusion quite similar to hibernation. That this season is shorter than the one in the North is quite evident when the size of bass from both localities is compared.

The artificial fertilization of black bass has been a failure. Experiments followed the general lines of those practiced upon the trout. The eggs were obtained from the female bass, however, only after a great deal of force had been exerted. The male proved even more stubborn; it was impossible to obtain the milt from the living male. The experiments, which were both costly and unsuccessful, had to be abandoned. And yet, there is no other fish more worthy of cultivation, for the black bass has definitely proved its popularity. It is a hardy, healthy, prolific, and highly adaptable fish, and its game qualities have been lauded as being second to none.

The spawning period of the bass is variable, beginning as early as March in the deep South and extending to as late as July in the far North. It is difficult to differentiate the male from the female black bass except during the spawning period. Despite the impracticability of artificial fertilization and cultivation, the bass is truly prolific, the female yielding approximately one-fourth her weight in eggs—from 2,000 to 10,000 annually. The spawning habits of large and small-mouth are very similar; yet, in accordance with its natural habitat, the large-mouth usually spawns in marshy spots and builds its nest of small sticks near the roots of weeds or plants, while the small-mouth scoops out a nest in the gravel or sand.

The nests are built by the male fish a few days before he begins the actual courtship. He plays the part of a fond suitor, sporting himself before his chosen mate, at the same time moving her toward his nest. She goes toward the nest only reluctantly. Then the male determines whether the spawn have matured; if she is not ripe, he will drive her out of the nest and seek another mate. During the actual fertilization period the two fish swim in opposite directions, rubbing bellies as the female ejects the eggs for the male to fertilize. Often the eggs are ejected with difficulty, and it is necessary for the male to twist and nip his mate in order to loosen the spawn.

The process of egg-laying usually takes from twenty-four to forty-eight hours. To protect the nest the male stands guard, occasionally fanning the water with his fins and tail to prevent sediment from settling. He will not feed during this period but will attack anything coming in the vicinity of the nest. The hatching period varies from a few days to two weeks. The young fingerlings remain together until they have attained at least an inch in length. However, these schools do not necessarily remain about the parental nest for the entire period. The fish attain about five inches in length the first year and about a pound in weight the second, and this pound-per-year rate is normal thereafter. Naturally, although these habits and characteristics are typical, there are a great many variations in them under different conditions.

THE PIKE FAMILY

There is no more misunderstood family of fresh water fish than the several species of the pike. There have been two reasons advanced to account for this confusion. Some anglers claim there is a lack of accurate information regarding the different species and their distinctions; on the other hand, there is the conviction among all too many anglers that the proper name for a fish is the one most popular in the local community. Be that as it may, the fact remains that there is a definite need for an accurate, specific listing of the pike and of the fish that have come to be known as the pike.

The three divisions of the pike family, once they are known to the bait caster, are relatively simple to distinguish. Scientifically called Esocidae, or Esox, these three species include the pickerel, the great northern pike, and the muskalonge. The pickerel is likewise of three kinds: the Western or little pickerel, the Eastern or chain pickerel, and the banded pickerel. The so-called "wall-eyed pike" is really not a pike at all but belongs to the perch family.

The coloration and markings of any fish are, at best, a rather loose

and often faulty criteria for distinguishing them, and this is especially true in the case of the various species of pike. The markings
vary greatly throughout the sections where the fish are found, not
only among the groups, but even among the different individuals,
according to their food or environment. As in the case of the black
bass, the most certain, as well as the most accurate means of identification, are the scales. The muskalonge shows scales only on the
upper halves of the cheeks and gill covers. The scales of the great
northern pike are distributed over the entire cheek and the upper
halves of the gill covers, while the pickerel is fully scaled on both
cheeks and gill covers.

Despite the variety of names and classifications in the pike family, all the various species are physically very much alike. They
have a long, unelevated body, with a correspondingly long head.
The snout is flattened and protruding above a very large mouth.
There is an abundance of teeth, very sharp, on both jaws and on
the roof of the mouth, with a few smaller teeth distributed on the
surface of the tongue. The fin structure is very simple: a single
dorsal fin, made up of soft, often slimy, rays is situated far back on
the body and opposite the single, soft-rayed anal fin. The scales,
the distribution of which on cheek and gill covers has been noted,
are rather small.

The pike is found throughout the northern part of this continent
from the Ohio river to Alaska. He is common in all parts of Canada
and especially in the Great Lakes region, as well as in the small
lakes of the upper Mississippi river valley. He is not unknown in
Europe and Asia.

The pike family, in addition to being misunderstood in regard
to classification, has suffered unjustly at the hands of a certain class
of fishermen who frown scornfully at the mention of any of the five
or six species of pike. Bass fishermen, too, seem to scorn the lowly
pike, tolerating him only as a poor substitute when the bass are not
biting. And yet the many types of pike are all gamey and worthy
antagonists for any bait caster. His wicked-looking jaws indicate
his ruthless character and his savagery, his dash, and his determination are things that should not be overlooked by the angler seeking
a thrill.

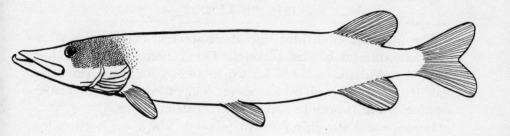

Great
Northern Pike

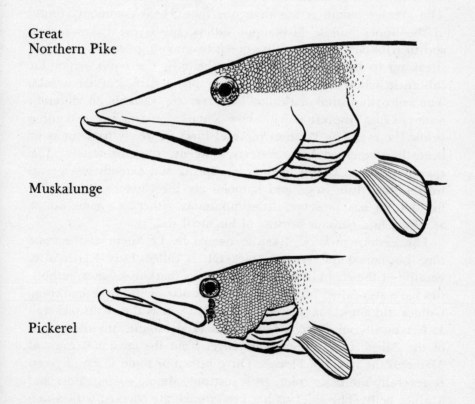

Muskalunge

Pickerel

Scalation of Cheek and Gill Covers

Diag. 7. The Pike Family

THE PICKEREL

The pickerel, subdivided into three species, includes the Western, Eastern, and banded pickerel. The Western pickerel, called Esox Vermiculatis, has been known to anglers for many years. He was described in 1846 by Le Sueur who called it "vermiculatis" because of the "wormlike" appearance of its markings.

In shape and size this Western pickerel, which has been called the little pickerel, is somewhat smaller than the others, with a slender body and a proportionally shorter head. His eye is rather large. The average length is less than one foot. He is commonly found in the upper middle Mississippi valleys, the Great Lakes region, and in tributary streams. Olive-green or grayish green—with a dark streak on its back and with a white belly—is the typical color for this little fellow. He is marked with many dark, curved streaks. The coloration and markings, however, are variable in different waters. Close inspection will show a dark, vertical bar extending below the eye. The Western pickerel lurks in weedy backwaters or beneath submerged logs, preferring weedy, sluggish waters. The spawning period begins in the early spring and extends for several weeks. Small fish, frogs, and tadpoles are the chief constituents of his diet. He has, however, little importance either as a game fish or as a food fish, perhaps because of his small size.

The Eastern pickerel, likewise named by Le Sueur at the same time he named the Western pickerel, is called Esox Reticulatus, because of the chain-like appearance of its markings. Later authorities have also called him Esox Niger because of the dark markings. Guides and anglers may point him out to you as the chain pickerel. It is typically an Eastern fish and is rarely found anywhere west of the Alleghenies, although it ranges from the coastal streams of Maine to the rivers of Florida. Olive brown or some shade of green is generally the basic color, with lustrous, almost golden, sides and a white belly. The sides, as has been noted, are covered with a network of dark lines and streaks, resembling a chain-like coat of mail. The dark vertical bar, present also in the Western pickerel, is found below the eye. The color of the fins is varied: the dorsal fin is usually plain, the lower fins reddish, the caudal fin marked with dark splotches.

Small fishes and frogs make up, for the most part, its daily menu. It usually attains a length of a foot to a foot and a half, although some two footers have been caught. Its weight is normally three to four pounds, seven or eight pounders being the exception, although they are on record. It spawns early in the spring, and its habits are typical of the family. There has been some dispute over his importance both as a game fish and as a food fish. He is, it is true, capable of giving the bait caster a fair amount of sport, even though he cannot compete with some of his brothers in this.

The last and, perhaps, the least important of the pickerel are the banded pickerel, recognized as early as 1788 by Gmelin. He named it Esox Americanus or "American Pike." Its range includes all the streams east of the Alleghenies, from Massachusetts to Florida. It almost duplicates the Western pickerel in characteristics of fin rays, scales, cheeks, and gill covers. He has been called the banded pickerel because about twenty curved black bars extend vertically. across the dark green ground color of his sides and back. The belly is white. To the vertical black bar beneath the eye is added a horizontal band extending from the snout through the eye to the gill cover. He is a very colorful little fellow, with reddish lower fins contrasting with the green and black of his body. It spawns early in the spring, and seldom grows over a foot in length. He is of no importance to anglers and has been described here only for the purpose of making a complete identification of the pike family.

THE GREAT NORTHERN PIKE

The great northern pike, often misnamed the pickerel, is the true pike (Diagram 7). Originally recognized in England and named Esox Lucius, it is the most extensive member of the pike family. He ranges over the northeastern United States and Canada, is quite common in the upper lakes of the Mississippi valley, the Great Lakes regions, and as far north as Alaska. He is unknown on the Pacific coast, but he is familiar throughout Europe, Asia, and some parts of South America.

Next to the muskalonge, he is regarded as the gamiest and also the largest member of his family. He has a long body approximately five times his depth, one fourth of the body being made up of his head. The snout is flattened, long, and projecting. Long, sharp teeth fill his jaws, and the roof of the mouth has a set of teeth which curve backwards. These villainous teeth and the cruel appearance of the great northern pike indicate his character truly, for nowhere is there found a more vicious killer, who will lurk under cover of weeds, ready to snap up any fish, frog, mouse, aquatic bird, or, in fact, any food that passes by. He is one of the greediest of all fish; many authorities contend that he will kill as much for the sake of killing as for food. He is certainly a cannibal, for he will attack even his own kind.

His coloring and markings are more reliable marks of identification than in the case of brother pike, for they remain constant under normal conditions. They are peculiar to himself, for his color is found in neither the pickerel nor in the muskalonge. His back and sides range from bluish through greenish gray, with the back darker and the belly fading to a silvery white. Light splotches of white or yellow cover his sides from head to tail in irregular spots.

A pike of fifteen pounds is common, and those of twenty-five to thirty pounds are not unusual. His value as a food fish is open to question. Some consider it highly palatable, while others despise it. True, the flesh is soft and rather dry, not flaky, but full of small bones. The flavor varies, depending upon the water the fish is taken from; cold water makes for a better tasting fish.

As a game fish, the pike is worthy of an angler's skill, especially when the fish weighs in the neighborhood of fifteen pounds. His fighting tactics are similar to those of his big brother, the muskie, although he tires quickly and usually gives in after a few bold rushes. The great northern is more important as a game fish to the Englishman than to the American, since America abounds in fish of a gamier nature.

He spawns, like the rest of the pike family, in the early spring, usually on a shallow, weedy bottom, in slow, sluggish waters. His favorite haunts are the slow stream or the shallow, weedy portions of large bodies of water.

Such is the great northern pike, a greedy cannibal, worthy of the bait caster's skill and very useful for filling in those times when bass and other game fish are not striking.

THE MUSKALONGE

Most important, and most exciting to the bait caster, of all the pike family is the crafty tiger of the lakes and streams, the muskie or muskalonge—scientifically named Esox Nobilior or Esox Masquinongy. He is looked upon as the gamiest fighter of all the large fresh water fishes, although there are many anglers who would give argument on this point. Regardless of the dispute, he is certainly the most vicious and savage member of the pike family.

Tales of this brute can be heard in the Great Lakes region, throughout all the northern part of the United States, and especially about the lakes of northern Wisconsin. His body is long,—about one fourth of this length being his head. The head itself is flattened, and has an underslung, projecting lower jaw. His teeth are the most imposing of all the pike family's: the lower jaw is fortified with several long bayonet-like teeth about one-half inch to an inch apart; in the front part of the lower jaw are a few, very sharp short teeth, while above these, on the upper jaw, are three clusters of fang-like teeth standing above the smaller, typical pike teeth. In addition to this array, there is a row of small, sharp teeth on the upper lip, and further back in the mouth, extending from the fangs to the throat, are three rows of recurved, very sharp teeth.

Markings and coloration in the muskie vary, environment and habitat seemingly exerting little or no influence. These colors run from dark grey and greenish to brownish shades, the back always being darker than the light sides, and the belly being white. Dusky spots cover the fins, while the lower fins and caudal fins show reddish tinges. It is in the markings, however, that the muskie shows the greatest variations. The young fish are characterized by small spots, but as the fish matures these grow larger, often changing shape until they form broad vertical bands.

He has been called many names—tiger, shark, wolf, etc.—to tell of his fierceness as the marauder of the waters. He thrives on fish, frogs, snakes, young aquatic mammals, and water fowl, but it is said that nothing in the shape of food will miss him. He lives alone, being a solitary freebooter, hiding cautiously among the water plants and rushes along the edges of streams, or beside rocks and banks in clearer lakes. From his hide-out he darts forward upon the unfortunate prey with his jaws wide apart. Unbelievable is the number of fish that this devourer can consume in a single summer,—good sized fish at that.

The period of spawning takes place early in the spring. The eggs are deposited in very shallow water, and the female's spawn numbers from one hundred thousand to three hundred thousand eggs. However, the frogs and turtles eat a great number of these. The eggs are rather small, about one-tenth of an inch in length. They hatch in about two weeks.

It is only when the muskie has attained a weight of about twenty pounds that he exhibits his characteristic ferocity and gameness. He will make furious dashes, usually diving for the bottom and the weeds if the bait caster does not hold a taut line. His endurance is the chief feature of his fighting tactics, since he cannot compare with many of his small brothers in cleverness. He swims in swift, straight lines, unable to double back like the bass or trout.

The habitat of the muskie during the summer is little known, for, as the water becomes warmer, he will go to greater and greater depths, feeding only early in the morning and late in the evening. It is during the teething period that he is perhaps the hardest to catch, because the muskie, being one of the most savage of fishes, strikes hard, but during this period it is almost impossible for the big fellows to do more than nibble at the lure.

Pugnacity, savagery, and endurance, combined with twenty to forty pounds of brute strength—that's the muskalonge, the true king of the pike family and a real test for any bait caster.

PIKE PERCH

It is well to include here the paradox of the pike family, the so-called wall-eyed pike, which, strangely enough, is not a pike at all, but a perch. A Dr. Mitchell first named him Stizostedion Vitreum in 1818, from the word "vitreous," because of his glassy eye. Hence the name "wall-eye." Nevertheless, he is truly a member of the perch family with nothing particularly pike-like in his form or habits, aside from the fact that he has a large mouth and teeth similar to those of the pike. Universal adoption has been given to the two names "wall-eyed pike" and the more correct "pike perch."

The wall-eye abounds in the waters of the Great Lakes region, throughout Canada, and the lakes of the upper Mississippi. He is built with a slender, trim body and an average sized head. His mouth, as mentioned earlier, is large and filled with many teeth, some of which are unusually long and sharp. The eye is characteristically large and glassy. Its perch ancestry is shown by the two well-separated dorsal fins and forked caudal fin. The scales are generally small with a rough surface. Both cheek bones and gill covers are spiny. A variety of colors is displayed by the wall-eye, olive or greenish-brown predominating. He is marked with mottled, rather indistinct lines and yellow blotches. The head is colored much like the body, while the underparts and lower fins show a pinkish or yellowish tinge. The first dorsal fin is quite plain, while the second fin and the caudal fin are mottled like the body.

His habitat varies with the time of year, since he migrates from the shallow waters over the sand bars and reefs to the cool depths as the heat of summer approaches. A rocky, sandy, or gravelly bottom seems to be preferred, in clear, cool water. It is here that he lies during the heat of the summer, sallying forth only to feed in

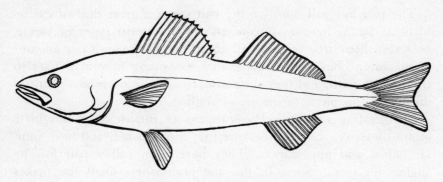

Diag. 8. The Wall-eyed Pike

shallow water on minnows, frogs, and other forms of aquatic life. He is not a solitary swimmer but lives in the company of other wall-eyes. He is seldom found alone. This makes him easy prey for illicit spearing and netting.

Early in the spring he seeks shallow waters in order to spawn, usually choosing a sand or gravel bottom. The eggs measure about twelve to an inch, each female depositing some fifty thousand of them. The fish moves on, though, to deeper waters immediately after spawning.

The wall-eye hardly ever exceeds three to five pounds, but occasionally you will hook one that is almost double this weight. As a food fish he is excellent, possessing a delicate flavor with firm, flaky white meat. He is a good game fish, rising eagerly to bait, fighting when hooked. He exerts an unusual pull for a fish of his size, and exhibits a peculiar type of tactics. When hooked, he does not dash, but swims rather slowly, pulling and tugging on the line. Simple as it may sound to land one, the beginning bait caster must handle the wall-eye carefully. The wall-eye is, nevertheless, an easy fish to catch.

The whole picture, therefore, of the pike family and those that have come to be known as pike, is a simple one once it is detailed. The three pickerel—Western, Eastern, and banded,—the great northern pike, and the muskalonge—not to forget the paradox of the pike family, the wall-eye or pike perch—are not only an interesting group of fish, but are also game that will test the skill and knowledge of every bait caster.

PAN FISH

The pan fish will not give the bait caster a great deal of excitement as far as fighting is concerned. On certain types of tackle, however, these little fellows will afford the fisherman a fair amount of pleasure. They are the game that the young fisherman likes to try his luck with, and they certainly provide a good means of introducing the neophyte to the art of angling.

Disregarding scientific classifications, we can describe this little group under one heading because they are all small and have similar habits and appearances. They have been called pan fish by anglers for two reasons: in the first place, their small size makes them exactly suited for the pan, and, in the second place, their flavor, when they have been browned over a fire, makes them a favorite with everybody.

Although there are numerous small fish that will come under this all-inclusive heading, it will be necessary to know only a few of the more important ones. Among these are the blue-gill, the sunfish, the crappie, the rock bass, and the yellow and white perch.

The blue-gill, more properly called the blue sunfish, for he is a member of the sunfish family, has a wider distribution than any other member of his family. From the Great Lakes to the Mississippi valley, from Texas to Florida, this game little fellow is known and enjoyed. He has a medium-sized, well-shaped head, with an unusually deep body, the depth of which varies from one-half of its length to its whole length. The body is compressed, almost flat, with a blackish ear flap. From the name we can expect its coloration to be some shade of blue; nevertheless, this blue varies from a purplish to a greenish hue. Variations are found not only in different localities, but also between old and young fish. It is commonly darker along the back, while the belly is almost copper colored. The young fish are generally colored more brightly than the adults, and they are likewise more beautifully marked with silvery glints and chain-like patterns. Its adaptability rivals that of the black bass, for the blue-gill will live happily in pond, lake, or stream. Very small minnows, minute aquatic organisms, and insects and their larvae constitute his favorite foods. Like most fish, he spawns in the spring or early summer. He is properly a pan-fish, because his length seldom exceeds six or eight inches, except in rare instances when it attains a foot. The blue-gill usually lives in schools; where one is found, there are certain to be others. His favorite habitat is the open water about sandy or rocky bars.

Closest relative of the blue-gill is that favorite of every young fisherman, the common sunfish. This is the "sunny" and the "pump-kinseed," popular with fishermen of every age. In range, the "sunny" extends from Maine to Florida, and from the northern part of the Mississippi valley northward to the Great Lakes region. His body is shaped like a pumpkin seed; hence his nickname. He has a small mouth, with large eyes set in his wedge-shaped head. For sheer beauty of coloration the sunfish is unrivalled among fresh water game. Yellow and blue seem to be predominant shades, the back showing a dark bluish color, paling through various hues to a light color on the sides and yellow blotches covering the whole body. The belly is a bright orange-yellow. Even the cheeks and fins are brilliant: the cheeks are yellow with blue streaks, the rays of the dorsal fin blue, with yellow membranes, the ear flaps are black edged with red, and the lips are blue. He shows a decided prefer-ence for vegetation and cover; an excellent locality to find him in is one surrounded by weeds and vegetation. Like the blue-gill, the sunfish's spawning habits are typical of his family. Insects and their larvae, minute crustaceans, and the spawn of other fish are his diet. Usually his length is from three to six inches, with a maximum growth of about eight inches. Unfortunate is the fact that he is so small, for certainly he would be one of our more important game fishes were he larger. The eager, pugnacious spirit that prompts him to bite at almost anything makes him the gamiest little fellow for his size that can be found. His courage, especially during the spawning season, is unrivalled among his or any other family, and this ability to take care of himself contributes toward making him one of the commonest of the pan-fish.

The crappie, often confused with the calico bass, has been called all kinds of names throughout the localities where he is found. He is a member of the sunfish family, whose range follows the Ohio and Mississippi River basins from Kansas as far south as Texas, although he is found more abundantly in Kentucky and in some of the nearby southern states than farther north. Its body is somewhat thinner than that of the other sunfish, with a large mouth and a projecting snout. This projection is partly due to an indentation near the front part of the eye. The eye itself is large, and

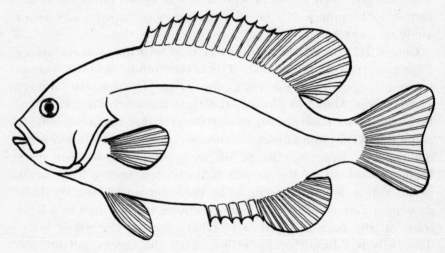

Diag. 9. Rock Bass

the jaws are covered with a thin, almost transparent, membrane. His dorsal fin has but six spines, while the calico-bass has seven such spines; it is by this distinction that the fisherman can tell he has a crappie and not a calico-bass. The crappie is a large fish for its kind, growing usually to at least ten inches, and often a foot in length. Olive green with a silvery tinge is the characteristic color; darker shades are mottled across the back. The lower sides and belly are silvery and are likely to appear translucent. The fins are colored like the body, only in darker hues. A golden border surrounds the iris of the dark eye. The crappie's habitat closely approaches that of the large-mouth black bass, favoring still, weedy ponds, and the spots around sunken trees and brush. The crappie's feeding habits are similar to those of the other pan fish, with minute aquatic organisms, larvae and insects, as well as the spawn of other fish making up the major part of their food. Like the blue-gill and the sunfish, it lives in schools and loves to congregate about some sunken or submerged object. His popularity is due not so much to his gameness, for, once he is hooked, he does not struggle to any great degree, but to his willingness to bite at any hour of the day or night.

Half-breed of the bass family—for it is neither bass nor sunfish, but a combination of both—is the little pan-fish known as the rock bass (Diagram 9). Originally found only from Lake Champlain southward through the Mississippi Valley to Texas, it is now common east and west of there because of transplantation. Its general appearance is similar to that of his big brother, the black bass, with the minor exception of having a deeper, more compressed body. Its mouth is large and filled with teeth, some of which are very sharp. The eye of the rock bass is large. The markings are black, forming indistinct lines along the olive-green sides. The name red-eye has often been applied to him because the iris is scarlet. It prefers rocky spots and clear cool water, and a school of these little fellows can often be found congregating on a rocky or gravelly bar. His habits of spawning are like those of the black bass. His menu consists chiefly of crawfish, small minnows, and insect larvae. He is found weighing from a half pound to a pound in most streams and often attains two pounds when taken from lakes. His value as a food fish is very great, especially when the angler finds him in clear, cold water. The rock bass, when taken from these cooler waters, will also put up a good deal of fight. He is a game little fellow with his large strong fins and his habit of curling up against the strain of the rod. This habit makes him all the more sporting for the bait caster.

Although these are the more important of the pan fish, it might be well to mention that such a classification is equally applicable to other little fellows such as the yellow and white perch, the calicobass, the warmouth and many others. So long as men continue to practice the art of angling, this group of little fishes will hold a respected position in their hearts.

CHAPTER VI

THE SPORT OF BAIT CASTING AND FISHING

BAIT CASTING practice organized as a competitive game has become during the past few years one of our most popular sporting activities. Although they are quite often referred to as "dry land fishermen" or "park fishermen," these earnest devotees to the sport of fishing enjoy advantages which more than make up for such "kidding." The practice not only increases the skill of the individual but also brings him in contact with many expert anglers. Bait casting during the off-season answers the same purpose for the fisherman that skeet shooting does for the hunter.

Several years ago the beginner could not hope to take up tournament casting, mainly because of the necessity of buying an expensive casting outfit and because of the time required for gaining the necessary skill in order to compete with the experts. Naturally, this kind of tournament casting did not attract the average fisherman. It was too expensive and had little of the practical side of fishing connected with it; it only taught one how to use tournament equipment.

Until recently the average fisherman could not expect to enjoy the off-season practice that the golfer or the skeet shooter might. The only opportunity the fisherman had of improving his casting technique was under actual fishing conditions, and under these circumstances the fisherman is usually concentrating on the fish. But a short time ago the idea of a skill game for the average bait caster was conceived. The game is known as SKISH, formerly called Fish-O.

SKISH

SKISH may be used for fly fishing also, but the description given here applies only to bait casting. The game practically duplicates fishing conditions by involving equipment almost the same as a bait caster's outfit. The reel must be a level winder and the line must not be under a nine pound test. Following are the rules and regulations governing the game of SKISH.

Rod—Unrestricted.

Reel—Must be of standard manufacture as regularly supplied by their makers, and sold by them through their regular channels, and fitted with level-winding device. No additions of any description will be allowed under these rules.

Line—Must be of strength test not less than nine pounds, and each contestant must submit his line for official test before casting in any recognized event, which shall consist of lifting any official 9-pound weight with it from the ground or platform. This makes eligible for use the new N.A.A.C.C. official 9-lb. test tournament line easily identified by its alternate red and white braid.

Weight—No casting weight or plug shall weigh in excess of $5/8$ ounce. The official N.A.A.C.C. casting weight is recommended.

Casting—Single-handed only.

Scoring—Three casts at each of ten targets will be scored as follows: Five points for a perfect on the first cast. Three points for a perfect on the second cast. Two points for a perfect on the third cast. If casting weight falls on or within the circle the cast shall be scored "perfect." If casting weight falls outside the circle, it will be scored "zero." No fouls will be allowed except for outside interference.

Targets—Ten targets consisting of ten rings, not to exceed thirty-inches in diameter, scattered at random, shall be anchored at distances unknown to the caster (clubs having at their immediate disposal but five targets may rotate contestants from targets one to five). No target shall be at a distance greater than eighty feet, or at a distance less than forty feet from the casting point.

Method of Casting—Free style unless otherwise specified. Caster will rotate casting at targets from one to ten, and as caster moves to next casting position, next caster will take the position vacated. Each target has its own casting point, thereby allowing ten players to be casting at ten different targets at the same time. (Clubs having at their immediate disposal but five targets may rotate contestants from targets one to five, and again from one to five, provided that targets numbers one and five are set at different distances.) No caster will vacate position just completed until caster occupying next position shall have completed his third cast.

Determining Winners—The caster having completed the necessary thirty casts (three casts at each of ten targets), and having the highest number of credit points shall be declared the winner. The caster having scored the next highest number of credit points shall be declared the runner-up, etc., etc.

Deciding Ties—In the event of two or more competing casters finishing with the same number of credit points, the caster having made the greatest number of perfect initial casts shall be declared the winner. Should, however, a tie still exist, then the total number of perfects made by the tied contestants in second casts at each target shall be considered in determining the winner. Only after the above determination has failed to break the tie will contestants recast or cast off for position.

Note: Some clubs have found it advisable for contestants to cast in pairs, the scorer of each pair to follow the twin play across the five separate casting points. The first pair of casters alternates in making three casts at the first target before moving on to each of the remaining targets. It is obvious that the scorer does not require a discriminating eye since only hits count and anyone can record hits and misses. Some clubs use just one scorer with only one 30-inch target and vary the casting points from 40 to 80 feet.

TOURNAMENT CASTING

There are a great number of casting and angling clubs throughout the country, nearly all of which are associated with the National Association Angling and Casting Clubs. These clubs sponsor various programs, but one of the interesting phases of their work centers around tournament casting. Following are the rules recognized by the governing body under which the bait casting events are run and which apply to tournament bait casting:

Reel—reels of any manufacture may be accepted for accuracy bait events only.

Line—unrestricted, except in five-eighths ounce event.

Weight—officially adopted by the association.

Casting—single-handed only.

Scoring—if the casting weight falls on or within the thirty-inch circle, the cast shall be considered perfect. For each foot or fraction of a foot away from a thirty-inch ring, a demerit of one shall be made. The final score shall be arrived at by subtracting the total demerits from one hundred.

After a caster steps into the box to make his cast, he is responsible for the results and must take for his score whatever he makes. No fouls will be allowed unless outside interference takes place. In no case shall a caster be given more than ten demerits on any one cast.

Three-eighths ounce and five-eighths ounce accuracy events shall consist of casting at rings.

Target Distances—five targets, consisting of thirty-inch rings, scattered at random shall be anchored at distances unknown to the caster.

No target shall be at a greater distance than eighty feet, nor at a less distance than forty feet from the casting point. The line used in the five-eighths ounce accuracy event shall not be less than nine pound test, officially adopted by the association.

Note: On any casting line it is permissible to use a loop or tracer not to exceed three inches in length, attached to the weight. Casting at rings as directed by Captain.

DISTANCE BAIT EVENTS

Rod—unrestricted.

Reel—free running without click, drag, brake, spring, or abnormal device or adjustment which would tend to retard the movement of the spool.

Line—unrestricted.

Weight—officially adopted by the association.

Casting—single-handed only.

Method of casting and scoring—the casting in this event shall be done on the lawn. Contestants each to make five casts in turn, one cast at a time, length of cast to be computed from casting point to where weight falls. Reckoned in feet, the sum total of the three longest casts, divided by the number of casts, shall be the average, and shall constitute the score of the contestant. If line or leader breaks after casting weight has left its starting position at the tip of the rod, the cast shall be scored nothing. After a caster steps into the box to make his cast, he is responsible for the results and must take for his score whatever distance he makes. No allowance will be made for breaking or other accidents after he is ready to cast. Casting shall be done from the casting point, and if contestant oversteps the casting point or line in making his cast and before the casting weight falls to the ground, there shall be deducted from the length of such a cast one foot for each foot or fraction of a foot so overstepped. The longest single cast shall be a matter of record. If it is impossible to secure suitable and accessible lawn for this event, it may be cast on the water, provided adequate provisions are made to assure accurate measurements. The official weights used in tournament distance bait casting are three-eighths ounce and five-eighths ounce.

THE SPORT OF FISHING

It was not so many years ago that fishing—in this country, at least —was a necessity, a means whereby early Americans provided themselves with necessary food. With the coming of civilization and its attendant exploitation of nature, however, fishing turned into something entirely different. The fish became scarcer, streams and lakes were no longer clear waters that ran through the wilderness, and fishing for food was practiced only on the far frontiers. Whether civilization itself is good or evil does not concern us; rather, we are concerned with the alarming results of man's thoughtless destruction of the fish and their habitats in his zealous conquest of the wilderness.

It is true that as far back as 1653, when Izaak Walton first published his "Compleat Angler," a few of the wiser people in the world took a rest from the turmoil of politics and business "just to go fishing." These few saw in fishing something more than the prosaic *business* of catching fish—though that, in itself, is an enjoyable occupation. In that day, however, there was no such problem as the one that faces the angling enthusiast of today, for there is a problem—in fact, a two-fold one. The angler today must not only learn how to use his tackle skillfully, but also he must learn that, unless the streams are restocked, there will be no more fish.

Figures that the United States Bureau of Fisheries released during the year 1938 show that, during the year, there were almost 7,500,000 licenses issued to fresh water fishermen. This was an increase over previous years. Just as there are more fishermen, however, there must be more fish.

"Conservation of fish population," all too many fishermen have said, "is for the other fellow." But conservation is no more the other fellow's task than it is yours. The purchase of a license does not give liberty to wilfully and wantonly kill as many fish as the license holder can get his hands on. If such a practice continues (and these words actually describe a few of our so-called "sportsmen"), the result will be that our fish population will be so quickly and completely depleted that government agencies such as state fish hatcheries will find it unprofitable to continue their good work. Well stocked streams and lakes will then be found only on private grounds and fishing as a sport for millions will be lost.

When you go fishing, you invariably go as much for the enjoyment of nature, for the satisfaction of handling rod, reel, and line skillfully, as you do for catching fish. The sportsman—if he can be called a sportsman—who tramps his thoughtless way through the woods, destroying what nature has taken years to build, fishing ruthlessly with the sole object of catching as many fish as possible, is doing his best to destroy the sport of fishing. When the inevitable result of his callous selfishness comes about, we shall see the end of fishing as the sport of millions and the end, too, of that greatest of all sportsmen, the experienced angler.

There are throughout the entire nation a number of Izaak Walton leagues whose purpose it is to guard against that result. If you are a man who loves the out-doors, who loves fishing as a recreation, and who believes in the ideals that the original "compleat angler" set up almost three centuries ago, then it is your duty to join a local chapter of the League in order that those ideals may be preserved. Conservation is not an individual enterprise. No one man—nor ten—can possibly hope to make it a reality; but when every person who knows the thrill of fishing joins with others to contribute his bit, then—and then only—will the dream of conservation come true.

While golf and tennis and all other similar games are what might be called man-made sports, fishing is a sport that only nature herself makes possible. And just as man has made certain rules governing his games, so has nature made a set of rules for the one she controls. The forfeits for violations of rules often mean the difference between winning and losing a game of basketball or hockey, but nature has set a much higher forfeit for violation of her rules. Unless man begins to follow a program of fishing very different from the one he has been following, he will pay the supreme forfeit of giving up the game itself. For fishing, if present practices continue, will soon become impossible for the many who now enjoy it.

The "fish-hog," who finds pleasure in his sport only when he has caught a sufficient number of fish to make the eyes of his companions "pop out of their heads," is perhaps the greatest offender. He is not fishing for sport, nor is he fishing for food; he merely wants to "put on a show" for his friends to satisfy his vanity and his "ego." The athlete who takes undue advantage of his opponent or who fouls deliberately is condemned by all men. Why, then, is the "fish-hog" not likewise condemned?

Turning from the sober side of the sport, we can see that the rise of its popularity as a national recreation proves that fishing is a most pleasant experience. The love of outdoor life and the desire to fish are the natural inheritance of every American. The development of skill in handling tackle, the thrill of catching fish, and the enjoyment of our natural resources combine to make fishing one of the happiest and most enjoyable of all leisure time occupations for everyone.

To keep the sport flourishing let us follow a few simple rules: 1. Know the state regulations for the waters in which you are fishing. 2. Obey the regulations. 3. Don't keep any more fish than you can actually use for food, no matter what the law permits. 4. Be a sport in the kind of tackle you use. Give the fish a fighting chance. 5. Handle carefully the fish you return to the water. Be extremely cautious in removing the hook from the fish. 6. Be careful in casting. Don't take a chance on hooking your companion. 7. Treat your fishing equipment carefully and it will serve you well on many fishing trips. 8. Fishing is a recreation which can be enjoyed during one's whole lifetime. Not only for the sake of future fishermen, but for your own pleasure in years to come, do your part in the conservation of our fish.

Whether you are eight or eighty, expert or beginner, remember that fishing, like every other sport, has its rules and restrictions. May your hours spent in bait casting be filled with luck and enjoyment!

INDEX

ANGLEWORM, 35
Artificial bait, 30

BACK-LASH, 3
Bait, 30; artificial, 30; deep running, 34; natural, 35; pork rind, 34; semi-surface, 32; spinners, 35; spoons, 35; surface, 32; weedless, 34; weight, 27
Black bass, 40-45
Blue gill, 54

CASTING, 1; flip cast, 12; grip, 2; left-handed, 12; night, 27; overhead, 6; side cast, 11; thumbing, 3; wrist action, 4
Construction of rod, 15
Crappie, 55-56

DEEP running bait, 34
Distance bait casting, 61

EQUIPMENT, 13; gaff, 23; leaders, 23; light, 23; line, 14; net, 22; pliers, 23; reel, 14; rod, 13, 14; stringer, 22; tackle kit, 22

FISH-O, 58-62
Flash-light, 23
Flip cast, 12
Fresh water game fish, 39; black bass, 40-45; muskalonge, 50-52; northern pike, 49; pan fish, 54-57; pickerel, 48; pike family, 45; pike perch, 52-54

GRIP, 2
GUIDES, 15, 21

HELGRAMITE, 36
Hooking, 26

Hooks, 28

KNIFE, 22
Knots, 28
Knots in line, 21

LANDING fish, 26, 27
Large mouth bass, 40-45
Leaders, 23
Left handed cast, 12
Level wind reel, 17
Line, 14, 20; care, 21

MINNOW, 36
Muskalonge, 46, 50-52

NIGHT casting, 27
Northern pike, 49

OVERHEAD CAST, 6

PICKEREL, 48-49
Pike family, 45
Pike perch, 52-54
Pliers, 23
Pork rind, 34
Pumpkinseed, 54-55

REEL, 14, 17; anti-back lash, 18; care of, 19, 20; level winder, 17; no thumb, 18, 19
Retrieving bait, 25
Rock bass, 57
Rod, 13; bamboo, 14; care of, 16, 17; construction, 15; length, 16; solid steel, 14, 15; styles, 15; tubular steel, 14, 15; weight, 16

SEMI-SURFACE BAIT, 32
Side cast, 11
Skish, 59-62

66

INDEX

Small mouth bass, 40-45
Spinners, 35
Spoons, 35
Sport of fishing, 62-64
Stringer, 22
Sunfish, 54
Surface bait, 32

TACKLE KIT, 22
Tackle knots, 28

Thumbing, 3
Tips on fishing, 24; hooking, 26; hooks,
    28; landing, 26-27; night casting, 27;
    weight of bait, 27; when and where,
    25
Tournament casting, 60-61

WALL-EYED PIKE, 52-54
Weedless lures, 34
Worms, 35
Wrist action, 4